Bus Love

Stories of Life and Adventure with the VW Bus

Tales collected by Tom Brouillette

Bus Love Stories, Philadelphia, Pennsylvania

Dedicated to the hundreds of thousands of original owners
of our fine VW Buses—without their purchases we wouldn't
have these beauties to tool around in now.

Bus Love: Stories of Life and Adventure with the VW Bus

Stories and illustrations © Copyright 2023 by the individual contributors.

Edited by Tom Brouillette

Cover art by Jean-Paul Jacquet

Layout by Taylor Joy Sanderson

ISBN: 979-8-218-26579-3

Bus Love Stories Publishing
P.O. Box 56277
Philadelphia, PA 19130

Email: BusLoveStories@gmail.com

Contents

Introduction *Tom Brouillette* • 7

Forward *David Eccles* • 13

Acknowledgements • 15

Microbus Memories

Better, Best, More Better, and Most Bestest *John Lago* • 19

School Colors *Howard Pitkow* • 29

Spirit of '76 *Kristen Caven* • 30

My First Drive in a Bus *J.P. Henriksen* • 40

Mid-Life Crisis Bus Story *Michael Kluckner* • 41

The Family Bus *Raffi Minasian* • 61

VW Busing Today

— Finding a Bus —

Kombi at the Crossroads *Tom Forhan* • 71

Truth & Beauty *Rick MacCornack* • 75

Daily Driver Delusions *Everett Barnes* • 80

The Treasure Bus *Keith Price* • 88

Bus Farming in Rhode Island *J.-P. Jacquet* • 90

— **Living with a Bus** —

My Childhood *Flash qFiasco* • 97

I Almost Bought a Conversion Van *Michelle D'Amico* • 102

Our Anniversary *Marek Zebrowski* • 106

All That Plus Evidence of Other Struggles *John Lago* • 110

Driving Tips: VW Buses & Sub-Zero Weather *Tim Rundquist* • 113

Tired of Life? *Rainer Müller* • 115

Wimpy, Wimpy, Wimpy! *Lois Grace* • 117

The Novel Solution *Chris Pollard* • 121

I Was Hauling In My Bus One Day *Clara Williams* • 125

One December Day *Jim Bryant* • 127

The Shape of Busing to Come

The New Microbus *Dan Proudfoot* • 133

Very Wild BUS *Stewart Alcorn* • 137

Bus Phantasmagoria

Night of the '54 Barndoor *Ron Van Ness-Otunnu* • 143

SPLAT! *Stewart Alcorn* • 151

The 5th Van *Ken Wilford* • 156

The Stories Behind the Stories

The Origin of the VW Bus *Dan Proudfoot* • 165

Author & Artist Biographies • 171

Glossary • 183

Suggested Reading • 185

For Nomi

Introduction

I'M A LATE BLOOMER. I didn't get a driver's license until 1981, when I was 30 years old and living in Boston. That year, I was offered a barely-running 1962 VW Beetle for $250 with the words "They're so easy to work on. You can fix anything yourself." I bought it, but I didn't have a clue how to fix it. After spending $1500 with a local foreign car mechanic—who joked to my roommate when he called to say my car was done: "I know he wants basic transportation, but this is ridiculous."—I finally had a car that worked. (After that kick in the wallet, my do-it-yourself mechanical knowledge went from 0-60 in short order.) With learner's permit in hand, I learned to drive with that Bug. After about a year-and-a-half, the already rusty Bug had even become *even more rusty*—I could see the road beneath my feet as I drove. So, I spent another $250 for a ratty (but fun!) 1963 Beetle convertible, and stripped the '62 of all usable spare parts. (Owning an old car, I learned that having available spare parts was a Very Good Thing.) At this time, I earned my living as a furniture mover, and occasionally friends asked me to help with their moves. After a crazy experience using my convertible Beetle to move a couch balanced precariously over the back seat with the top down, it occurred to me that there must be a better way: What about a VW Bus?

In the early '80s, there were still quite a few old VW Buses in and around Boston, but having dealt with rusty Beetles, I wanted something better than the rusty ones I was seeing. It was rumored by my co-workers that good Buses were to be found in California, and for $2000, which was exactly my budget, I could do very well. In October of 1984, I flew to San Francisco, stayed with friends, scoured newspaper classified ads, and wandered the streets looking for a Bus. I only found beat-up ones that would need a lot of work to even drive, or very nice ones that weren't for sale. I gave up. On the last day of my two-week sojourn in California, I rented a car and drove

The editor in the grease-stained shirt by which VW Bus owners are known, and The Bakery Bus, 1986.

to the Napa-Sonoma wine country. On a whim, I bought a local paper to see if anything was to be found in the classifieds. There it was: a 1966 Deluxe! For $2000! It turned out to be a European-market, blue-and-white sunroof model, brought over to the States from Switzerland in 1974. The VW emblem on the front was removed and the logo of the owner's shop was painted on it: The Sugarhouse Bakery, St. Helena, Calif., with a picture of a baker rolling out dough. It was *almost* love at first sight: *How do I figure out the kilometer speedometer? Why are there no bumper guards? Why doesn't the radio play FM?* (It was an original Blaupunkt European radio made for European frequencies, including short wave). Even the headlights and taillights were European spec, and different. I didn't realize what an unusual and *cool* Bus I had. It brought appreciative comments everywhere I went ("Nice Bus!" ✌), and the first hitch-hikers I picked up were two young women from Germany traveling around California (I interpreted this as a good omen). On my way back to Boston, I visited my parents in Illinois and brought them together via the Bus (divorced many years, they had not seen each other in over two decades). Our lunch was awkward, but this gathering went a little way to healing a wound in my life, and hinted that this vehicle *brings people together.*

In the early 1980's, old VW Buses were cheap and at the bottom of their depreciation. In fact, once I had bought my first Bus, people would stop me to say they had one to get rid of—to take for *free*. I was given five or six in the space of just a few years— usually running, but sometimes not. I found new homes for these Buses, and the new owners were delighted to have them. On the streets of Boston (and, I'm sure, almost everywhere else in the world), there were still Buses driven by passionate-about-their-ride folks as "basic transportation," and the camaraderie was alive and well. We would wave to each other as we passed on the roads. We would stop and chat with other owners whenever we found them getting in or out of their sometimes raggedy, but still running, Bus. It was a unique fellowship.

A local Bus owner placed an ad in a national VW magazine about his wish to get nearby Bus owners together, and I jumped at the chance. On a February day in 1986, I met with five other enthusiasts to share stories and exchange spare parts. That was the beginning of our club, NEATO: Northeast Association of Transporter Owners (the term "Transporter" is one of the official VW terms for its line of passenger and commercial van-like vehicles). We soon started a newsletter dedicated to owner-ship of vintage VW Buses, and as one of the editors of *Old Bus Review*, I met and corresponded with hundreds of enthusiasts in the US, Canada and overseas. Many of these folks became close friends as we experienced the joys of owning and operat-ing these storied vehicles.

As letters, stories, and photos for the newsletter poured in every month from the far corners of the globe, I began to realize that there may be no motor vehicle better suited to motivate peo-ple to enjoy life on the road. Certainly none have appeared to inspire so many owners to write tributes to their motoring expe-riences. As author John Lago writes, "experiences that would not have happened while driving any other vehicle." Writer Dan Proudfoot adds "No other vehicle can match its power in producing smiles among passersby of all ages."

Although relatively few of these vehicles are still driven daily, more are being resuscitated and restored every year. A large community has bonded over their shared love of vintage Type 2's (another official name that Volkswagen gave them) at shows, campouts, through scores of clubs, and via the internet. Buses

that would have previously been sent to the crusher years ago
are lovingly resurrected. Times have changed from the days of
cheap, even free, VW Buses. Restored or original specimens
now command prices of *many* thousands of dollars. It's even
possible to build an almost perfectly anatomically-correct Bus
from entirely new reproduction parts and sheet metal. The current economics of owning and maintaining a Bus have pushed
them out of the "basic transportation" category.

The VW Bus in popular culture often shows drivers and passengers as carefree hippies. Though there's an element of histor-
ical truth to the stereotype, it misses the richer and deeper story
of VW Busing. *Bus Love* reveals the VW Bus owner as resilient,
creative, resourceful, mechanically-vigilant, patient, and phil-
osophical—and with a vehicle like this, you've got to have a
sense of humor!

In the first section of this book, *Microbus Memories*, several
authors recount childhood or first experiences with Buses
owned by family or friends in years past. *VW Busing Today*
reflects the trials of finding and keeping a VW Bus. In *The
Shape of Busing to Come* are stories of conjecture: what will
the VW Bus mean in 25 or 50 years? And in the section, *Bus
Phantasmagoria*, are tales on the edge, imaginings that could
be plots for *The Twilight Zone*. The final article "*The Origin of
the VW Bus*," reveals details of the inspiration and design of
the Type 2, giving credit where it's due. Most of these stories
appeared over the years in *Old Bus Review*, some have been published elsewhere, and a few have never been published before.

All but one of the stories in this collection feature VW Buses
1967 and earlier, before the major body style changes of 1968
and 1979. That was the original focus of the club and newsletter.
My alternative title for this book was *The Varieties of VW Bus
Experience, Volume One*. "*Varieties*" because you'll hear a wide
variety of voices in the stories ahead. "*Volume One*" because as
long as these vehicles still roam, the adventures and stories will
keep coming. I hope that *Bus Love, Volume Two* will contain stories of more recent Type 2's—and with the new-fangled all-elec-
tric ID. Buzz now on the market—perhaps a new generation
will have new adventures and write new stories.

As I mentioned in the first sentence of this introduction, I tend to be late with things. This book, for example, was first suggested in the 1990s. Since then, a lot of life happened, and I realized getting this book published was now or never. Though much of the book is of a "time," I believe the timelessness of the stories shows through.

Meeting and corresponding with the authors and artists in this book, and many others at shows and gatherings, my life has been enriched beyond measure. The VW Bus, indeed, *brings people together*.

Ready to ride? Then hop in, get comfortable, and enjoy this collection of stories of life and adventure with the VW Bus.

—*Tom Brouillette*

Forward

MY RELATIONSHIP WITH VOLKSWAGEN BUSES started way back in 1976. My wife, Cee, and I had decided to travel overland to Kashmir and the Himalayas before the security blanket of job and mortgage descended, and were looking for a suitable vehicle. A Land Rover was the initial choice but they were so… spartan. Then Cee spotted an ad in the local paper, "1967 VW Camper for sale. Fully equipped. Fast cash sale needed. £500." Thirty minutes later we were looking at a lovely red and white Canterbury Pitt VW Camper, complete with sink, folding cooker/grill, bench seats round a dining table and a bed! Perfect—our own home on wheels! The woman selling it was edgy and evasive and we did the deal there and then. She wanted us to take it immediately and promptly unloaded mounds of stuff from inside, handed us the paperwork and said "Be happy." It was sometime later we discovered she had split with her husband and was, unknown to him, disposing of his assets before he returned from work to collect them!

That little VW took us through Europe, Turkey, Iran, Afghanistan and into Pakistan and India. In six months, we covered 30,000 miles, and the only problems we had were one puncture, and a dodgy starter motor solenoid. Oh, and of course the pulling brakes after we hit a massive pot hole (we never did fix that, we just learned to steer left when braking!). It was our window, our refuge, our haven.

When we returned to England in 1977, we had to sell the Bus to raise money. Watching someone drive our home away was gut-wrenching. However, two years, two secure jobs as teachers, and two children later, Cee once again spotted an ad: "VW Camper ready to go. Reluctant sale £550."

Our lives were complete again. It was a 1967 Devon Camper and when we collected it the seller's children were crying. I knew how that felt. For the next 20 years that Bus took us and our three children on holidays all over Britain and Europe. In 1990 I joined the Split Screen Van Club (initially just for spare parts, which were impossible to find back then) and found a community of people who, although from all walks of life and backgrounds and ages, shared a passion for living with a VW Bus. When in '92 I took over editing the club mag, I soon discovered this community extended all over Europe and North America (and in fact the world!). Tom B. was editing the NEATO club mag around this time, and we soon struck up a friendship, which has continued ever since. Nowadays, I edit *VW Camper and Commercial* magazine and the Bus tends to be more show and display use.

I am often asked what the attraction of owning and living with a vintage Bus is. No other vehicle conjures up quite the same emotional appeal as a VW Bus, even now children always smile and point at "the car with a face." There is no one answer— but several of the seemingly infinite reasons have been brought together here, in *Bus Love*. Enjoy.

—David Eccles

David Eccles is author of:

VW Transporter and Microbus: Specification Guide 1950-1967, 2004.

Campervan Crazy: Travels with my Bus: A Tribute to the VW Camper and the People who Drive Them, 2006.

Traveling With the VW Bus and Camper, 2007.

Air Cooled VW Bus and Pick-Up: Special Models, 2011.

VW Camper – The Inside Story, 2020.

VW Camper & Commercial (magazine), Editor

Acknowledgements

In addition to thanking the contributors to this book, I want to mention people behind the scenes who did the work of keeping NEATO and *Old Bus Review* on the road. I particularly want to shout out to:

Peter Albarian (president), George Bossarte (membership secretary), Bill Bowman (president), Jim Bryant (treasurer), Dave Easterwood (editor), John Foley (editor), Rob Laffoon, 1957-2019 (editor), Mike Motta (founder), Marek Zebrowski (president).

Additional thanks are due to many people who helped push-start this book down the road to publication:

Special thanks to Marek Zebrowski who so long ago suggested the idea of this book. Without his inspiration, prodding and kind advice, this book might not have been.

Thanks to Burt Reif, Michael Müller and Norbert Scheunemann for help with translation of text from English to German and German to English.

Thanks to Melanie Pratt of the Split Screen Van Club (UK) for helping me find a long-lost author.

Photo of the editor in the Introduction courtesy of Lee Smith.

Photo of 1951 Bus and Porsche 356 courtesy of Drew Ogden.

Photo of editor and Nomi at New Jersey Pine Barrens Trail Bash by Matt Cuddy.

A Bus-load of gratitude to J.-P. Jacquet for cover art.

Gratitude for Taylor Joy Sanderson's help in formatting this book—her assistance pulled me out of a nosedive of despair.

Several readers gave their time and insight to this book: Kristin Caven, Joan Kocsis, John Lago, Flash qFiasco, and August Tarrier.

Love to Rachel Martin, my life-support while putting this book together, and who helped me get it over the finish line.

Microbus Memories

Better, Best, More Better, and Most Bestest

John Lago

AT A CERTAIN POINT IN SIZE, what was designed as ticket becomes baggage. What had been growth goes to tumor, satisfaction drops down into pride, and use and beauty becomes so badly bloated that whole civilizations collapse, buried by a successful effort to turn creation into trash. In times wayback the Romans went this way with just about everything, more recently the French did it with bread and cake, while our thing is, periodically, with cars.

Remember the cars of the Fifties? Who could forget the '59 Cadillac in particular and anything put out by the Chrysler Corporation in general? Hoo, the length of those things! And the weight and the mass. And then when you factored in those ridiculous fins—I mean those *finnns*—a viewer was not able to escape the feeling that the design for these monstrosities grew out of some sort of wrestling match between one committee wanting to build an airliner and another wanting to build a submarine. Lawd, Lawd.

Some said it was World War II in the Forties and the Korean War a little later. They said we were plain up-to-here with war effort, and the way to set such a thing in balance was with an equal effort in the name of peace. Factories that formerly cranked out planes and tanks were retooled to make cars. An America on the march became an America on the move, and what better way to move than in a car, your car, good today, better tomorrow, bigger next year, so big the year after that they outgrew everything except anticipation of next year's model which was expected to have more of everything, including size. Instead of naming them fittingly, like the Chrysler Zucchini, the 98 Yard Oldsmobile Ocean Liner, the Cadillac El Dorado-Gold-Mine-Smelter-Slagpile-and-Toxic-Waste-Dump, they were called the "Chrysler Imperial," the "Olds 98," and in the case of the Cadillac, simply the "El Dorado."

Back in those days size mattered. It wasn't just the cars. It was also the kids. It seemed like every living parent wanted one huge car and at least two fat kids. If you were a kid back then, you barely had time to brush your teeth because your parents were always stuffing food in your mouth. "Kids are starving in Korea," was the explanation, and you were not allowed to rebut with "But I'm full," if only because you were not allowed to talk with food in your mouth. Open wide, kick back, pork up. Exercise? Exercise was equated with stress, stress was reminiscent of war, so everywhere you went you took the car. The car was fed too. More iron, more glass, paint, wax, fat of the land in the form of oil, more power, more size. Ticket becoming baggage, a butterfly going back to a grub, feeding, falling, fattening on a bloated image of good, better, best, more better, and most bestest.

The end was near.

Kitty-corner and across the street from the house where I was pretending to grow up was a neat yellow house owned by the Langes. There were three Langes. Mr. Lange, Mrs. Lange, and a tawny work of perfection named Barb. To ordinary and sub-ordinary neighborhood primitives like me and Ricky and Gary and Jimmy, she was God's living artwork. She could paralyze us with a glance. If she spoke, we would collapse and would need several days in isolation to regain normal function. Nobody had to tell us what love was. It was kitty corner and across the street.

To keep Mrs. Lange and Barb in a state of comfort and security, Mr. Lange went to work every morning and came home every night. You did that back in the Fifties. There was a lot of social and inner pressure to make certain promises and then hang around and keep them. In the Fifties, a job was your second identity. Right after the introductory "How do you do?" usually came the question, "What do you do?" To ask Mr. Lange such a question was to hear, "I have recently acquired a dealership in import cars."

Barb didn't know it, but the day I gave her up for a new love was the day Mr. Lange drove home in one of his imports. You could hear him coming. Unlike the silent-running monstrosities of the other neighbors, Mr. Lange's import entered the neighborhood audibly. His entrance had a catchy sound, even in the distance. You knew it was the sound of a motor coming, but how to describe the effect on your ears? Was it a peppy and sassy mechanical song, or would you want to be more figurative in your description and call it the sound of fun coming to a dull party? Regardless, it was a sound worthy of investigation. I was outside at the time, on a ladder reluctantly painting the trim on the front of the house, so I was in the perfect position to get an eyeful of the vehicle bringing this new sound into the neighborhood.

It was a little Bus, of all things, red and white, with lots of windows and hardly longer than two bikes in tandem. Mr. Lange was in the driver's seat. He looked enviable there. No right-minded teenage kid should envy a balding middle-aged businessman, but there I was, enviously watching him pass in the peppy and sassy sounding little Bus. He let off on the gas, nimbly wheeled it to the curb fronting his house, and stopped. His first steps out of the Bus seemed like dance steps and did not seem inappropriate. My ears still held the sound of the sassy motor, but somewhere in the distance was the sound of busy chisels as epitaphs were being carved on tombstones for the Chrysler Zucchini, the Oldsmobile Ocean Liner, the Cadillac-El-Dorado-Gold-Mine-Smelter-Slagpile-and-Toxic-Waste-Dump, and many fitting others.

Ask My Uncle

"You have to wonder why the Germans didn't do it this way in the first place." He shook his head and went on with, "I mean, what the hell. They start two world wars, right? And for what? To dominate the world? Sorry boys, it doesn't work that way. You want to dominate the world you have to offer something people want to accept, not something they have to resist. Ask my uncle. They buried him in Normandy. I saw his grave."

There were nods from both of us then, solemn nods in respect for the powerless sent off to die by the powerful, and then it was back to business.

"They'da done it right my uncle would probably be alive and driving around in one of these right here instead of lay'n dead over there. I mean, when you give it a little thought, doesn't it make more sense to go to work than to go to war? Somebody wasn't thinking."

There was no argument in that. If there was any argument, it was over the selling price. We were standing in front of his four-year-old Volkswagen Microbus: according to him my offer was too low; according to me his price was too high.

"I'd like to come down, but they hold their value. There's no planned obsolescence in these things like with American cars. You can buy this Bus today and a year from now you can sell it and get almost all of your money back."

"What if I don't want to sell it?"

"That's what I mean. There's not much of a turnover so they hold their value. You don't drive this once around the block and lose $500 like you would with a Ford or a Chevy."

We were getting to the stage of pauses. Initially the conversation was breezy and without much interruption—me stepping in with, "I was wondering about that Bus over there," and him responding with, "Let's take a look at it."

The Bus was standing alone, the "For Sale" sign in full view from the road, and as we took the few steps necessary for a closer look, he rattled off a description. "It's a '62, only four years old, just broken in, really. She's solid, tight in the front, new tires, never been hit. Here's something for you," he said, stopping by the driver's side, opening the front door and ceremoniously shutting it. "See? Solid. Nothing tinny here, nothing cheap." He opened the door again and said, "Try it yourself. It's all quality workmanship."

From the front door we went to the passenger side and stopped at the cargo doors. Those doors too, he said, were works of precision, and when he swung them open, he made an expansive gesture to the inside as if he had just opened the doors of a warehouse. "Look at all that room. Nine passengers or one ton of cargo. One ton. These little Buses are actually rated to carry a full 2000 pound load."

Closing one door and then the other, he nodded meaningfully and three steps later we were at yet another door. This one was low on the back. It was hinged on top, and when he flipped it up, the space inside revealed a motor. "Here's where true German engineering comes in. Everything about this makes sense. You get real traction with a motor in the back. Also, with the weight back there, the Bus steers like a dream. She's front-light, and that takes all the pressure off turning the wheels. Go ahead, take it out on the road." He put the keys in my hand, put his own hands in his pockets, and stood there grinning.

When I came back, he didn't wait for me to offer an opinion. As soon as I stepped out of the Bus he said, "How about that transmission? Isn't that an easy clutch? Do you know that *Motor Trend* voted VW the smoothest shift on the market today? It's all synchro is what it is. You can drop from fourth all the way down to first with hardly two fingers on the stick."

He had more, and circled the Bus as he went into detail. Independent front and rear suspension. Never a problem with a water pump or radiator because the motor was air-cooled. Flat glass throughout. "Break a window, no big deal. Look here, even the windshield is two flat pieces of glass. No distortion, easy replacement. I don't even want to *know* what it costs to replace some of the fancy windshields you see on cars nowadays."

It wasn't just the Bus we talked about. There were other things. In the small time it took the sun to put light on the earth at a slightly different angle, we had the opportunity to compare notes on wars fought by one born yesterday and one born today, and came to see that today is mostly yesterday in disguise. At a time like this a person sees value in giving, so when I drove away in the little Bus, one person was satisfied with the sale and the purchase, although an observer trained not in history but in math would have insisted there were two.

Look at an Egg and See a Bird

What is held in the mind ends up in the hand. You have a thought or are hit with an impression, and soon it has an address and a telephone number. Each time you call or visit, you bring food. What is born as possibility grows into probability, and to complete the deal from the abstract to the real, all you need is time.

Much time had passed since Mr. Lange first entered the neighborhood in his little red and white Bus. And even though Mr.

Lange had long since left the neighborhood and so had I, the impression of his entrance stayed with me. It had an address and a telephone number and each time I called or made a visit I brought food. "Here's a few more bucks for the Bus," I would say after cashing another paycheck. Cashing a paycheck was incomplete without putting Bus money aside. It was a savings thing. You always have money for what you spend it on first, so the first bite out of every paycheck went into what I called "Bus tokens." From the abstract to the real. In time possibility became probability, and soon, instead of saving for a Bus, I had a Bus.

By then, Buses were everywhere. You have to remember that the Split-window Volkswagen Microbus was the original van, the original minivan, and the original "camper." When introduced, there was no other vehicle like it. Not one. At that time there was no Chevy Van, no Ford Aerostar, no Plymouth Voyager. The closest competition was a thing put out by the Big Three called a "panel truck," which was a big-nosed, overweight hearse look-alike reappointed to haul anything you could possibly throw, shovel, or stack in the back: big, small, dead or alive.

The credit for the concept of the VW Microbus goes to a Dutch businessman named Ben Pon. During a visit to a factory in Germany where the production line was hatching out early models of the Volkswagen Beetle, he saw something. On the factory floor was a vehicle of a different order. Strictly for use in the factory, it was called a "platform truck," and was fashioned from the floor pan and parts of the Beetle but put together in such a way that workers could efficiently move just about anything from one end of the plant to the other or to any place in between.

Since Ben Pon was one of those rare souls who could look at an egg and see a bird, he saw something in the platform truck that went way beyond mere utility on a factory floor. Soon he had a rough sketch in a notebook that would set into production a vehicle dubbed the "Volkswagen Microbus." (See "*The Origin of the VW Bus*," page 165) For more than 17 years its body style would be basically unchanged. People would call it "ugly" because of its boxlike configuration. Other people would call it "cute" for the same reason. Later, it would have names like "The Early Bus," "The Split-window Microbus," or just plain

"The Splitty," owing to its windscreen, which was two flat pieces of glass set almost eyelike above the dash and giving the Bus a sense of a personality tucked somewhere within and needing only close human association to bring it out.

And close human association caught on quick. Production was not able to keep up with demand. Which was probably one of the reasons Mr. Lange's first steps out of his Bus looked like the steps of a happy dancer.

Another reason had to be the sheer fun of driving. It was not possible to park your ass in the front seat of a Split-window Volkswagen Microbus without having fun. Even before turning the key you knew your driving experience was not going to be ordinary. The feeling was immediate because the driver's seat had you sitting high in the saddle and way, way up front. You were sitting so far up front, in fact, that you were actually cantilevered ahead of the front wheels. You were not relegated halfway back to the trailer hitch and stuck behind the mechanical opacity of eight feet of blinding grill, fenders, and hood. No. The driver of a Bus did not exist as an afterthought in the design of the vehicle. In his Bus he was positioned like an eye in a head, and was first upon the scene of things unfolding, and by this position was encouraged to look, and to look again, and to keep on looking until his perception went beyond the jaded realm of "to look" and into the fresh realm of "to see." Fun.

Adding to the merriment was the steering wheel. This thing had the same general shape as any other steering wheel, but soon you could see an added, 'nother function, and this function—like the seat—had a lot to do with placement. The steering wheel on a Bus was situated nearly horizontal. Sitting in the driver's seat, you were behind a steering wheel tilted only a few degrees off level. And since it was not a high steering wheel, but posted slightly above your lap, it invited you to lean. You could drive sitting upright in the seat, fingers wrapped around the rim in conventional fashion, or you could slide those fingers up around the frontal curve. This encouraged you to lean forward and rest the belly of each forearm on the curve to the lee. Here, you're even closer to things unfolding. Your eyes are inches from the windshield, and they are there comfortably. Leaning, you take some of the weight off your buns. In appreciation, your buns stay awake. Some of their burden has been shouldered by your elbows, and this particular brand of happiness can translate all the way to your fingers which are not only doing duty on the front rim of the steering wheel but also poised directly and naturally above the dash and therefore tempted to playfully tap out a response to the notes and riffs sent up by the rolling rhythm of the road.

All this you find out right away. What you find out a little later is that drivers of other vehicles think your Bus does not belong on the road. They would like to show you where it does belong, but for that you would have to bend over. Why would their feelings be thus? "It's a traveling roadblock," you often hear, or, "A dead man can grow toenails faster than you can drive that Bus." Someone else will weigh in with, "I could pass you up with a wheelbarrow," while his buddy might add, "In a race with turtles and snails, that thing would come in third." All exaggerations, but all there to offer evidence that the Split-window Volkswagen Microbus was a creature genetically under-equipped to indulge in the kind of torque-inspired mechanical temper tantrums capable of smoking the rear tires to the point where they turned the road into a scene cut from a bad hair day in hell.

It was the motor.

The same motor that gave you 30 miles to the gallon gave people behind you the fits. Interpreted literally, the motor in an early Splitty had a displacement of 1200 cc (cubic centimeters), and an output of 36 hp (horsepower). But to those behind you, the "cc" translated to "cheese curds" or "chocolate chips," and the hp to "hamster power" or "hamstrung puppies." The four little cylinders made the Bus slow off the line, shall we say "patient" going through the gears, and shall we say "hesitant" to embrace highway speeds without a tailwind or a downhill assist. Even moderate uphill grades and ordinary headwinds could have you slowed to the point of quickly collecting vehicles in your rear-view mirror. On a two-lane blacktop with lots of curves, hills, and yellow lines, it's been said an Early Bus could back up a line of traffic from Cairo, Illinois all the way to Bumph Uque, Egypt.

The motor.

To keep pace with the traffic on an American highway, the motor needed double the horsepower. To spring from one stoplight to another in a way to satisfy the cars to the rear, it needed twice the torque. Still, during the time it was used in the Split-window Bus—from before 1950 to the end of 1967—the motor remained basically the same. Over the years a few more horses were added here, and a little more torque tacked on there, but during the seventeen-plus years of pushing the Bus it seemed a thing confident in its originality, unchanging, like a natural born leader, or like someone too far off the beam to know that the person standing inside his own skin is irretrievably insane.

The insistence of American motor traffic convinced many drivers of Early Buses that keeping the motor small was insane. These were times when truckers were being paid a nickel a mile. Some drivers got six cents, but it was generally a nickel a mile, with no laws restricting miles-per-day driven or hours-per-day driving. Truck drivers hated Splitties. There was nothing quaint about getting caught behind a Bus when every missed opportunity to pass was costing them precious pennies. To register their discontent it was customary for them to follow with their radiator kissing-close to your rear window. To look back made you feel like a hood ornament, only sweatier. When they'd finally get a chance to pass, you'd get the air horn and the finger, and when they'd pull ahead, they'd deliberately swerve to the shoulder so the right-side tires on the trailer would ride onto the gravel and kick up a shower of dust and stones, much like a dog kicking shit on the one who holds the leash.

People in passenger cars weren't losing a nickel a mile, but that doesn't say they weren't above losing their tempers. Back then, the posted limit on highway speed was 65. Back then—but not only back then—that number was understood to be the minimum speed. If you wanted to talk maximum, 72 was the top if a cop was in sight, but if not, people who drove 72 got passed up. The top speed of an Early Bus was 59. So you can see what's at work here. If a speed between 65 and 72 is "regular," then 59 is "constipation." Buses equaled blockage. People passing without encountering interference treated you as a mere annoyance, but to have to wait for an opportunity to pass could push them beyond merely annoyed all the way to pissed off. And if they had to pick a number for an opportunity to pass—that is, if they were approaching a line of 300 cars backed up behind your Splitty and they had the distinction of being car number

301—by the time it was their turn to pass, they would go from pissed off all the way to furious. They would grimace and careen, lean on the horn and pass you like a kidney stone, driver and passengers pumping mono-digital salutes and exploding into that special kind of profanity that blisters the chrome off your door handles and leaves no doubt as to who is their object of desire in all their fantasies involving sex and violence.

So most drivers of Early Buses learned to take the roads less traveled. Whenever possible, the Splitty driver chose roads that held off demands and instead posed questions. Questions like: Is most of speed just a rush to a time of no value? How much value is there in a time where, before you even get there you already want to be somewhere else? Would you rather have a sense that life is a thing emerging or that life is an emergency? If it's true that all things come to pass, and if it's true that the present is where we spend our entire life, is it also true figuratively as well as literally that speed kills?

The little motor, basically unchanged. Built small to show that most of speed is for those who have not yet arrived. Kept small as a reminder that to wrestle with synchrony and seasons is not much different than rowing out in a leaky boat onto a deep ocean with no water, to fish with a frayed line for a big fish that isn't there.

School Colors

Howard Pitkow

I SAW A VOLKSWAGEN BUS for the first time when I was in 5th grade. I think the year was 1964. The Viet Nam war was going strong. I remember studying it and bringing in the color maps from the *Evening Bulletin*. Kennedy was already gone, and Johnson was the President.

We had a contest to pick the school colors for a flag. We were instructed to pick two colors that went "nice" together. The best combination would win.

I used to daydream often in school. I was bored at times. "Not working up to full potential," my mother used to hear. I was staring out the window and something caught my eye. I had never seen anything so neat in my life, so far. It was a Volkswagen Bus. Two-tone: green and white.

I immediately wrote down these two wonderful colors. They were very different than the rest of the class. No one else used either green or white in their choice.

My teacher approved. He thought I had quite an imagination. He told my mother that I had artistic talent. I never told him the reason I picked these colors. The school flag was to be green & white—all due to a split-windshield Bus.

I have loved these cars ever since.

Spirit of '76

Kristen Caven

HAD MY PARENTS ALLOWED ME TO USE A BLOWTORCH, Hoggie would have been my first art car. I would have welded a giant spring to the rear hatch to make a curly tail, and painted two black spots to imply snout-holes on the white vinyl cover of the spare tire mounted on the front. But I was only ten and didn't have such creative license just yet. At least Mom and Dad laughed at my idea. Dad even suggested we name our new '67 Sunroof Deluxe VW Bus "The Road Hog."

Hoggie came honking its stuffy-nosed horn into our lives one spring afternoon in 1975. My brothers and I raced to the front window to see what the beep-be-beep beep was happening. A boxy, green and white vehicle was trundling down the driveway like a giant planter box on wheels, with leaves and branches waving through the roof. "It's a greenhouse model," Dad called out to Mom, whose face showed a happiness that excited me. My father, whose name meant *forester* in another language, had expressed his own creative license by transforming our house on the edge of the Colorado prairie into an oasis. He had planted Russian Olives, Blue Spruce, an entire fruit orchard for the back yard, most of them started from sticks and cuttings. The day Hoggie came home, he brought home a king and queen maple that towered over the other trees the day they were planted.

Today any vehicle with sliding doors that hauls kids and trees from nurseries with such ease would certainly be called a mini-van, but Hoggie was a *Bus. Bus* is a much more communal word than *van*. A van is a service vehicle, something perhaps to carry praise-singing youth groups with good insurance and carefully monitored morals. A Bus is a bigger idea, something bigger than a company car, something you get on in good faith with a spirit of adventure and ride to wherever it's going. Even a Microbus. In the Summer of Love, Hoggie had still been brand-new, and it would always carry within it the rebellious romance from that year.

My brothers and I could feel it. We were planning to take our own magical mystery tour this summer—family-style. We heard our parents talking about exploring Indian mounds, crossing Lake Michigan on a car ferry, camping out in the Land of the Jolly Green Giant, and visiting places with unusual, beautiful names. Sandusky, I would repeat over and over in my head for weeks. Cahokia.

Mom used her creative license with Hoggie when she got a bolt of cream-colored cotton cloth featuring red and blue fife-and-drum players. The ragged little men and boys printed on the fabric wore tattered breeches and carried a flag twined with ribbons bearing the words Spirit of '76. The whole world was excited about the upcoming Bicentennial, Coloradans even more so, since our state would be one hundred years old. Everything was about 1976. Next fall, my big brother Cosmo, eleven months my senior, was entering seventh grade, and I the sixth. Seven, six. I would be independent from him for the first time as big (wo)man on campus at our elementary school, while he forged ahead as a lowly junior high sevvie. Oh, and I weighed 76 pounds.

Perhaps Mom felt something for those little figures on the fabric, whose job it would have been to keep time so the soldiers could keep going in the toughest of times. For weeks she planned and measured, folded and sewed, tacked and tied. Then one day when she picked us up from school, Spirit-of-'76 curtains hung on all of Hoggie's windows. The whole interior of the Bus had been transformed for our bicentennial odyssey with accessories like fabric trash bags, book bags and pillow-covers. Mom even made matching Spirit-of-'76 bandanas for herself and me. And lunch bags with those little fife-and-drum guys on them that we could carry through the last week of school to anticipate our trip, then again next fall and throughout 1976. Mom had made our Hog a home on wheels for our summer tour back East.

The night before we left, Mom and Dad wrestled the middle bench out of the Bus, which rather alarmed my two brothers and I. We kids had discovered that we could all stand up on the bench with the rag-top open and our heads out the top. Cosmo and I could comfortably rest our arms on the edge of the open roof and look down on the road and the world around us. Younger brother, Lemon-Lime could just see over the edge if he stood on tip-toe. But when we drove down Independence Road towards our house, all three of us bounced our crazy heads off and the wind pushed laughter back down our throats. Lemon-Lime, he could just fly. His bright red curly hair would whip straight up in the wind like the comb of a rooster. Once the wind currents blew a wasp into the collar of Cosmo's blowing shirt and stung him three or four times. Mom said that was it for roof-bouncing, but even while still welted and teary, Cosmo begged and whined with us to convince her that it was worth every risk.

Our parents had to explain to us that night that there was no point keeping our beloved bouncy-seat in, since we were put-ting a canvas car-top carrier on the roof and wouldn't be able to open it up anyway. We began to see new possibilities when they installed wall-to-wall carpeting, a colorful checkerboard pad mom had made by sewing carpet samples together. At last it became clear: the Bus was to become our traveling fort! When I crawled in, I saw new possibilities in the kid-sized scale of the interior, and gave my mother helpful suggestions on how we could arrange it. "This can be the kitchen over here," I said, gesturing to the area behind the driver's seat. I ran to get my toy sink and stove from my room.

But Mom stopped me. "Go pick out some books for the book box instead," she said, bringing out our old milk-delivery box from the garage. The box made a nifty seat for reading, especially with the Spirit-of-'76 covered foam cushion on top of the hinged lid.

Cosmo stretched out luxuriously on the back seat with his head on a pillow. "You can have the whole floor, Krissy," he announced, uncharacteristically generous. "Lemon-Lime, you can ride in the way-way back. You're just the right size."

The day of our departure, my brothers and I slammed out the back door right after breakfast, and climbed into our places. We talked about all the adventure that awaited us, the places Hoggie would take us. We would see some real dinosaur bones. We would play with cousins in Detroit and Ohio. We might even see Mount Rushmore, the mountain with the faces in it. Cosmo climbed in the driver's seat, knowledgeably working the pedals.

"The emergency brake is on, right?" Lemon-Lime asked him. For being just a little kid, he knew a lot about cars.

"Duh, Wilbur," Cosmo retorted. It was his favorite phrase, mocking anyone who dared tell him anything even remotely obvious. He pulled the lever back another notch anyway.

We waited. And waited. And waited. Finally, Mom came out to get us. "Get back in here and clear your places," she ordered. As we loaded our dishes into the washer, she ran down the packing checklists with us one more time. Then, she forced us to clean our rooms, no matter how much it pained us to do so when we were dying to get on the road.

Two hours later, the three of us were back in the Road Hog. An hour after that, I wandered inside again to go to the bathroom. Dad's Beatles record was playing on repeat in the living room. I stared at the pattern in the linoleum at my feet, where I could see faces sometimes. I wondered what Mount Rushmore looked like. I could hear Dad in his bathroom on the other side of the wall. I was about to flush when I heard my name. Instead I tiptoed up the hallway and stopped outside their bedroom door. When I peeked around the corner, I could see their bed, covered with my dad's clothes. Next to it, a neatly packed suitcase. My parents were around the corner in their walk-in closet/bath.

"Krissy's growing up, have you noticed?" My mother was saying in her quiet voice.

"No," my dad joked. "Say it ain't so." The toilet flushed. "I'm not ready for puberty," he said. I had no idea what that word meant, puberty, but something about it made my stomach pinch up. I crouched down.

"Maybe a few more years," said my mom. "It's just something about how she notices things now. She's more sensitive, I suppose."

"Great, that's all we need," my dad said. "Another sensitive woman in the house." The water came on. My mom said nothing. "I'm kidding," he said. I heard him kiss her, noisily.

"Can I get your razor, please," Mom asked in a flat sort of voice, "so I can pack up the toiletry kit? So I can close up my suitcase? So I can load it in the carrier? So I can close that up?"

My dad grunted absentmindedly, then spoke again. "I've gotta shave first," he said. Then I heard the shower go on.

"Is it okay if I pack up the kit," Mom said, "and you just put your razor in your pocket until tonight?" Tired. She sounded tired.

"We have some ripe tomatoes, don't we?" Dad called from inside the shower. "Shame to waste them. And that big banana squash, we should get it off the vine, don't you think?"

After a while, this is what my mom said: "We can wrap it in a baby blanket and give it to my mother when we see her, she doesn't think we have enough kids." Dad laughed really loud in the shower, like a bark.

I ran on tiptoe back down the hall, down the back stairs, closing the screen door softly so it wouldn't slam. Back on my checkerboard floor, my heart was pounding as if I had just done something bad. What the heck was puberty? My nose was back in my horse book when Dad whistled sharply from the deck. "Hey kids," he shouted down. "Why don't you go pick some tomatoes? The really red ones, we can eat them for lunch. If they're a little pink still, that's fine. Or even green. Yeah, get a whole bunch of them. They can ripen on the dashboard as we drive, and we'll eat one every day."

At twelve-thirty, my dad hollered from his bedroom that we should load up real quick and we could have lunch in Longmont, the next town up the road. By two, we were all starving. Mom had given all our perishables to the neighbor who kept the house keys, so she unpacked some cheese and bread from the old aluminum cooler and made us tomato sandwiches with the ripest of our garden trophies. Our first picnic of the trip was on a tarp on the back driveway, with cherries from our own tree for dessert. Lemon-Lime rocked back and forth on the banana squash, which was over half his size. Cosmo and I perched in Hoggie's open side door, kicking each others feet.

By four o'clock, I had finished my book. I went in again to find a new one. Mom called out, "Flush the toilet, Krissy." How embarrassing. She was helping Dad look for his keys. The phone rang. He answered it, then covered the mouthpiece and called at me as I went back down the stairs. "There's all those weeds right by the driveway," he said. "As long as you're hanging out in the car, why not pull a few?" At five o'clock he said, "Hey, as long as you're out there doing nothing, why don't you pick some cherries to take on the road?" Mom helped us pull the weeds. She got bowls and bags and helped us pick cherries. The screen door slammed each time she came back outside.

At six thirty, we finally pulled up the long driveway to the road above our house, and a few minutes later we were on the freeway heading east. Dad shifted gears, then reached up to touch his chin, said a swear word and told us he had forgotten his razor. He turned Hoggie around and soon we were driving back down our driveway. Dad said "I'll just be a minute," and left the engine running, but Mom reached over and turned it off. She sat there in silence and we all watched her for a long time. When she finally turned around there was a bright smile on her face. "Hey, let's sing a song, kids!"

We sang "I've Been Workin' on the Railroad," "Feelin' Groovy," and "Puff the Magic Dragon." Lemon-Lime made farting noises instead of saying "Puff." It was hilarious.

Dad came back, mumbling excuses for the long delay. "I couldn't find where I put it," he said, "and then the phone rang and it was... bla, bla, bla." Mom just sang louder and Cosmo made fart noises, too, like it was his idea in the first place. Dad started the engine and got Hoggie back on the road. He joined in when we sang "Shine on Harvest Moon," and "Bicycle Built for Two." We sang "Mary Had a Steamboat" and "Free to Be, You and Me." We got to Longmont just before eight.

A steer the size of a building stood guard outside the Sirloin Stockade Steak House. My father moo-ed at it and put Lemon-Lime on his shoulders, taking Cosmo's hand and mine, so he was full of children, he said. The sun angled its way towards the Front Range of the Rockies. Our adventure had finally begun! A real steak house! We had never been to a real steak house. The restaurant amazed us with its modern inventions: A serve-your-self salad bar and a serve-yourself ice cream dispenser. There were three colors of Jell-o in the salad bar—red, green and yellow. And chocolate pudding. One spout of the ice cream machine served chocolate, one served vanilla, and the one in the middle served both at once. Mom said I could serve myself, but I couldn't figure out how to turn the machine off and ended up with two pounds of ice cream balanced on my cone. Ice cream the size of a bas-ketball, Cosmo said. My dad said I could share it with him as a reward for finally getting out of the house. But he kept taking gigantic bites and throwing it all out of balance. "Today is the longest day of the year," he said, as we sat on a bench outside, staring at the blue mountains and the colors in the sky.

"Duh, Wilbur," said Cosmo, putting the last bite of his own neatly-twisted cone into his mouth. Dad gave him a little thump with his ice-creamy fist on his head.

Hoggie was nowhere to be seen, but soon Mom appeared with our toothbrushes. "Let's go wash up in the restaurant bath-rooms," she said, "then I have a surprise for you." Cosmo was embarrassed that someone might see us. Dad said people brushed their teeth in public restrooms all the time, but Cosmo frowned, like he didn't believe him. To me, the mint toothpaste tasted good after all that chocolate. Cosmo and Lemon-Lime said Dad said he needed a little more time in the bathroom, so Mom gave them the toiletry kit to give to him. Then she took us kids back outside.

The surprise was in the parking lot behind the restaurant. Hoggie had been transformed into a little house on an asphalt prairie. All of the curtains were pulled closed, and the inside was now a cozy bedroom. A sleeping bag was unrolled onto Cosmo's seat. He dove into it, saying "Mine, all mine." Mom said, "Do you remember when our family took a trip in the station wagon?" We did. We remembered whining and being hungry and tired. We never got on the road until after lunch, never got to our reserved hotels until midnight, and always had to go to the bathroom at the wrong time. I remembered throwing up french fries in the back of our station wagon. "Now that we have Hoggie," Mom said, "we don't have to rush to hotels. We can just stop and go to sleep when we're tired, and pack up and leave in the morning."

"Look." Lemon-Lime pointed to the oblong windows that ran above the curtained ones. "You can even see the stars." Lemon-Lime, just as Cosmo had decreed, was snuggled under blankets in the way-way back.

On the floor, two sleeping bags were zipped together. "Is this where the rest of us will sleep?" I asked, curious about the prospect of cuddling between Mom and Dad all night.

"No honey, just me and Daddy," Mom said.

My stomach pinched again. I struggled with my feelings but tears pushed into my eyes. My spot, granted by Cosmo's authority, was not mine after all. Did I suddenly not have a place in this family? Was it something I did wrong? Did it have to do with puberty?

Mom noticed my sad face and smiled. "You have your own bedroom, honey."

She drew aside the long Spirit-of-'76 curtain that hung behind the front seats to reveal a bed, just my size. A wooden plank rested across the space between the seats with a piece of fabric-covered foam on it. Some girls I knew had princess beds with curtains around them. I finally had one, too, but mine had a view, since the front windshield had no curtains. I crawled into my special room, propped my head against the door on my bedroom pillow, and felt like the princess of the Road Hog. Cosmo was even a little jealous. "You have a better view of the stars than the rest of us," he said.

I sat up for a long time watching the last reds and purples fade from the sky above the Front Range, which I wouldn't see for a long time. Like stars coming out one by one, snores came from the other side of the curtains. First my father's deep buzz from the floor. Lemon-Lime's little snuffle from the way-way-back. Cosmo's occasional snortle, and finally my mother's even breath. If I pointed my toes, I could touch the hole-dotted vinyl of Hoggie's ceiling. If I pressed my feet on the cold, hard steering wheel I could move it, even make the tires squeak a little, but I shoved my toes back under the blanket when I heard my dad's snore break up a little. The giant steer stood by the highway, a protective shadow between us and the headlights that scored the darkness. Up close, the dark shapes of the tomatoes stood sentry on the narrow dashboard.

I didn't ever want to close my eyes. Something new was coming my way. Adventure, change, mysteries, *something*—and I wanted to savor the feeling. I knew the summer would bring good memories, but at this point I could only imagine what they would be. My grandmother's face when she'd first see the new baby, then get the joke. The mushroom we would find in a campground, almost as big as the banana squash, that would stink up the bus when it got warm and my parents would give away to strangers. Our entire family would squeal "Wheeeeeee" like idiots when Dad turned off Hoggie's engine and coasted down long hills to save gas.

Later that year, the free love that filled the world the year Hoggie was new would change my family forever. Dad would fall in love with someone else while driving Hoggie around on a church errand. Soon after, my mother would leave him and go to a university somewhere near where the giant steer lived. In future summers, Mom would borrow Hoggie from my dad to take us kids on independent camping adventures during her custody month. The new stepmother would first take out the curtains, which she thought were tacky, then the carpet, which she said smelled, and finally insist Dad trade Hoggie in for a van.

But tonight, snores inside and stars outside the cold, protective windows, we were all at home, and all together in the wide open world.

My First Drive in a Bus

J.P. Henriksen

WHEN I GRADUATED FROM HIGH SCHOOL IN 1963, a friend of my fathers, Jan Hoowij (pronounced Yan Howey), asked for help moving to California from Corpus Christi, Texas. His wife had just had an operation, and couldn't sit for long periods, so he needed help driving one of his vehicles, a Volkswagen Bus! I don't remember the exact details, but it was a windowed Bus with semaphores. I can't recall ever having been in a Bus before that one, but we had driven Bugs during my high school days, including one episode where we drove in water so deep that the car floated sideways for a short distance!

Jan and I picked up the Bus from the Volkswagen dealer who had serviced it for the trip. Due to my inexperience with Buses, I didn't realize that I was sitting over the front wheels, so I cut the wheel, and drove right over a curb in the dealer's lot. Probably gave a few people a good laugh!

As we drove across Texas, New Mexico, Arizona and southern California, we were passed by lots of families in station wagons. In those days some wagons had a rear-facing seat for the kids in back, so when they'd pass by, I'd hit the left turn signal, and up would flash the semaphore, surprising the kids. We had a pretty uneventful trip to California, except for the fact that here I was, a 17 year-old from south Texas, going to the exciting L.A. area for the first time. When we got there, I met an old movie star from the thirties (Philip Dorn), and went to Disneyland, which was only a few years old at the time.

We always waved at other Buses, and they would wave back. I like to think that VW Bus drivers have always waved at each other. Driving a Bus is, and always has been, being part of a brotherhood that some other people just don't understand.

Mid-Life Crisis Bus Story

Michael Kluckner

Rekindled Desire

ONE DAY IN THE WANING MONTHS OF THE 20TH CENTURY, a man drove his Honda Accord to a warehouse in an industrial part of the city to get his cappuccino machine serviced. To his surprise, across the street was a storefront outfit called Bow Wow Auto Parts, a venerable dealer of all things Volkswagen, especially the "after-market" parts manufactured in places like Brazil and Mexico, that were considerably cheaper than the factory-made ones from Germany. In his youth a quarter-century earlier, he had spent more money at Bow Wow than at any place other than the beer store.

Lost in a reverie of long hair, greasy skinned knuckles and Buses up on blocks on the front lawn of his old rooming house, he started to climb out of the Accord when a vintage canary-yellow split-window Bus pulled up at the Bow Wow store, the noise of its exhaust vibrating the vintage fillings in his teeth. The driver's door opened and a young guy with short hair, a T-shirt and shorts jumped out and walked swiftly inside.

Seized by curiosity, he walked across the street, sizing up the Bus. Its yellow paint job met a line of body filler just above the rocker panels—the place where they all get cancer first. There was also some rust, obvious from the bubbled paint, at the base of its prow, right where the passenger's feet rested. That had been the undoing of his last Bus, the '65 with the home-made pop-top: the front of it was a million flakes of rust flying in formation. No stomping the feet in time to the music in that car, he thought, or you'd end up like Fred Flintstone in his stone-age runabout.

It was almost 20 years since he sold it and went sensible with small Japanese sedans, but he had once been a proud member of the Order of the Volkswagen Bus, taking the vows of poverty (by only owning stuff that would fit in the Bus) and utility (by knowing how to keep it running himself). Now he was dragged down by a complicated, busy life, and laden with unnecessary responsibilities and useless possessions, like a cappuccino machine. Could he recapture even a whiff of the unfettered joys of youth with its boundless future?

The Bus was a Kombi model, with three windows on each side. He peered in through them in the gaps between the bought-at-a-garage-sale-and-handstitched-by-somebody-wearing-baseball-mitts curtains. A large white dog slept on the floor, its body fitted amongst a scattering of tools and parts. The interior was paneled in cheap brown veneer, with a few stowage drawers and cupboards like a really tacky houseboat. A small fire extinguisher was bolted to the wall. The rear "bed" was a hinged seat set upright and ready for passengers, covered in thick foam with a stained cotton Indian print, matted with white dog hair, over it.

Perhaps the grandparents were driven to church in it on Sundays, he thought cynically. This was no camper, no Westfalia wonderbus for those happy family outings in the Tyrol, the Sound of Music playing on the eight-track. It was a hippie-mover that had somehow survived the catharsis of the last quarter-century.

Part of him recoiled from its primitive, grubby tackiness. The rest said, "this was once me." He had just walked around to the back of the Bus, noting approvingly the bumper sticker that said: "You'd Drive Better If That Phone Was Stuck Up Your Ass," when the owner emerged from the store, carrying a new muffler in one hand and a bag containing seals and bolts in the other. He was about 25, single silver earring each side, fairly clean-shaven, hair only a little spiky, striking blue eyes sort of like Paul Newman—a handsome young guy. Whip off the earrings and put a suit on him and he could be selling mutual funds to pensioners. He appeared mildly bemused by the older man. "Poor old fart," he was probably thinking, "nothing to do but relive his youth."

The man introduced himself, confirmed the first impression by saying he had had a Bus "just like this one"—he almost said "sonny" in a trembling Jimmy Stewart voice to the young man, whose name was Kevin—then suddenly heard himself asking if it was for sale. "Where did that question come from?" his inner voice asked.

Kevin's aloof demeanor crumbled just a little and he stammered, "...well, uh, I guess I...," before going mute. Regaining his composure, he zipped around the back and opened the engine cover, stood back and pronounced proudly, "It's really clean!" And it was, given that he had no chance to run out and get it steam-cleaned. A new coil, still with its Bosch logo visible, was attached to the fan shroud. There were no hanks of hair or pieces of finger or other greasy bits lying around. He had had it for four years, he said, and had the engine professionally rebuilt at a time "When I had the coin, man." Actually, he didn't say "man," as he was from the wrong generation, but the word hung in the air like a distant echo.

There was a little play in the front end, he said, that he knew would have to get adjusted. He asked Kevin how much.

"Uh, $4,000 —I couldn't let it go for anything less than that."

"I've got to think about it. I'll be in touch in a day or two," said the older man, adding an unspoken thought, "unless I have a sudden attack of common sense."

Just another amusing interlude in the life of the middle-aged, he thought as he drove home. Really, buying it was out of the question. The inside of the Bus was appalling —doubtless the scene of all sorts of sordid youthful rites involving people whose response to criticism or rules would be, "Hey, what's your problem, dude! People just wanna be free!"

The Next Day

Nevertheless, he thought he ought to check it out. The next day, he dialed Kevin's number. The phone rang a few times, then was picked up. A wall of guitar-rock sound, or cat-torturing, then a sleepy-sounding voice.

"Hullo?"

"Oh, Kevin, I met you outside Bow Wow yesterday, I'm interested in your Bus."

"Yeah, yeah…"

"Uh, could I come by tomorrow and look at it again, maybe drive it… ?"

"Tomorrow, umm... no, I gotta work late." He paused for a moment, as the ripping guitars in the background reached a frantic crescendo. "What about Thursday?" he asked. "I'll be home about 5."

"Perfect."

He gave the address, a street in a part of town that was "transitional," meaning it was hard to say whether it was going up or down.

In his Honda, he picked his way down a narrow street between two lines of parked cars, some of which had a complete set of inflated tires; it was a block with houses too scruffy to have attracted the yuppie restorers, so it sat awaiting an eventual apartment rezoning. Rents would be cheap. There, ahead on the left, was the Bus.

He parked and went up to the door of a small stucco house; on the stoop of the place next door, a glassy-eyed, stringy-haired man nodded acknowledgement. Or maybe he just nodded. Kevin's door was open, revealing a small living room. A poster taped to the wall advertised a rock band with an aggressive name. A pile of stereo equipment occupied one corner. There was a chair with ripped arms, a barbell in the middle of the floor, and a toolbox and a telephone on a little wooden table. He tapped on the aluminum screen door and a minute or so later Kevin emerged.

As he had the first time, Kevin went directly to the engine compartment and opened the creaky little door. "See, I got that new muffler on," he said. The older man walked around to the front of the Bus and lay down on the road where he could look up at the front suspension. Some new clips and clamps had been added to tie it together. Yes, there was some rust, but it didn't seem too bad.

He got the key from Kevin and climbed in over the wheel-well and skidded his bum onto the driver's seat. He'd forgotten, it was like being in a cave. If he bent forward just a little, he had a good view out the front and could see more or less okay out the sides, but the back window seemed to be in another county. The effect was heightened by the curtains, which permitted a few shafts of sunlight to penetrate into the dusty gloom. He was seized by the sensation that he was about to take a basement suite for a drive.

He turned the key, the starter whirred and, somewhere back behind him both spatially and chronologically, the engine burst into life. The VW air-cooled din—tin and fan noise and the drumming exhaust—was amplified in the coffin-like fuselage. And there was a smell. A muddle of confusing sensations swarmed up into his gut—it was the '70s again, he was in his 20s.

"Just wait a minute," Kevin said suddenly. "I've forgotten mah dog." They were back before he had done the whole H with the gearshift, remembering the long throws, the push down with the shoulder to get through the reverse-gear gate, and the peculiar clonking sound the gearshift made when it came out of reverse into neutral. The dog lay down amidst the tools and rubbish, happy to go for any ride at all.

He pulled forward, cranked the wheel to miss the parked car in front, and got it up to about 10 in first, the fan and engine roaring, then second, the road quite bumpy and poorly paved ahead. The Bus began to porpoise a little, waterbed-like. Another familiar sensation from long ago. Yet another sensation—he was sitting on top of the front wheels, like the weight on the end of a balance beam, moving up and down, up and down, being rocked.

The steering was truck-heavy, the steering wheel almost horizontal, and something clunked when he turned the wheel hard. As he drove along and got out onto a main street, he became increasingly aware of yet another sound, like gravel being stirred around in a coffee can. It got louder the faster the Bus went, so it had to be in the transaxle or the reduction gears. A problem.

A few more blocks and he had looped around and decided that the price would have to drop. Kevin agreed that it was something that would need fixing eventually, but said: "I'd just kick myself if I let it go any less." He had a girlfriend, see, and the two of them and Rover liked to go on camping trips, so... the older man just walked away.

The Search Narrows

A few weeks passed, during which the man busied himself with other things and only occasionally contemplated the equation: Bus = adventure = why not? One day, walking in a trendy part of town, he spied a candy-apple red, dropped, chopped, customized, mag-wheeled split-window Bus parked on the other side of the street, and felt it reel him in. He *had* to have a look. Is this where old Buses go now? To the customizers? It was about as far from Kevin's rolling doghouse as he could imagine. Taped into a side window was a handbill advertising a VW show in a suburb not too far from town, set for a mid-August Sunday. He felt it reeling him in, too, and resolved to go.

From the number of Volkswagens of all descriptions parked for blocks, he could tell he was approaching something unusual. He was amazed at how young the crowd was—the friendly, slightly nerdy quality of nice kids in their 20s. Most of the Buses were owned or had been restored by 20-somethings. But there was a camperized one (a '57) owned by a chubby, easy-going guy with a wife and few small kids eating bologna sandwiches on kaiser buns and drinking Coke from cans, half of them inside the Bus and half wandering around outside.

One young man, maybe staring 30 in the face, had a radical delivery Bus for sale and had printed brochures of it arrayed on a card table. The owner had cut the retaining wall behind the two front seats down to seat height, and wore the uniform of a modern Bus junkie: close-cropped hair that was a bit ragged as if cut by garden shears and tinted blonde or henna-red, an earring, a rather manic smile and intense gaze, a T-shirt with a VW logo, baggy shorts, and large sneakers, and he had a web site.

"Did you do the restoration?" the man asked.

"Yeah, but if I was gonna do it again, I'd go completely stock." He gestured at an old VW ad on his table which showed a line of identical red and white window Buses along a straight suburban street lined with identical red-roofed, white-sided houses.

"Why are you… like, I'm curious, why are you devoted to these old Buses?"

"Well, they're just totally cool... I grew up with them around and, like, there's the boxy shape and everybody turns to look at you as you drive by and..."

Another man, probably in his mid-30s and surrounded by a flock of little children, had come up and was listening to our conversation.

"It's cuz it's the most bitchin' vehicle on the planet," he said emphatically.

"The most what vehicle?" An especially loud dune buggy had roared by at the crucial moment in his epistle.

"Bitchin.'"

"Awesome," the first guy confirmed.

"It's like drivin' a work of art."

On the tarmac, the world had divided into air-cooled people and water-cooled people surrounding the new Beetle. Like the Deux Chevaux, the older man suggested to his new friends, referring to the cult-classic Citroen 2CV. They hadn't heard about it, but agreed that a good parallel was between Mac people and PC people; people with PCs were like people with normal cars with their radiators and water-cooled engines. Ordinary. On the beaten path.

Everything about these Bus junkies seemed different from those a generation before who moved about in them. They were fascinated both by antiquated Bus technology and the latest in high-speed computer and communication equipment, whereas the earlier generation, or at least some of them, was eager to go back to the land. Later, talking with his wife about them and their multifarious interests, he gave up trying to make the logical connections. There's probably a thread there that's invisible to us, she said. Like the thread that tied the VW to peace symbols and the antiwar movement, in spite of its Nazi origins, and was invisible to his parents.

The Quest Bears Fruit

Some weeks passed. It was now late-September: cool nights following beautiful Indian summer days. He had put up notices in a couple of VW-friendly garages: VW Bus Wanted, prefer split-window, and his telephone number, but had heard nothing. He had copied down phone numbers or ripped off the little tabs torn in the bottom of ads pinned to bulletin boards, but all were for more modern Buses, so he wasn't really interested in them, except trying to find out what they were now worth. Kevin had wanted four large for his beater, which seemed absurd given its condition, yet the owners of the fully restored ones at the show were asking eight. Twenty years ago, the last one he had owned, which admittedly was made of rust bonded together by paint, had cost him $800 or so. And the crew-cab Transporter his wife and he had bought in the late 70s from Eddie the stoned carpenter? Eighty or a hundred, max. It was a 6-volt but its wiring was so gummy it would only start with jumper cables and a 12-volt battery they dragged around with them.

He had just gotten back from a walk to the store.

"Oh good, there you are," his wife said. "You got a call from a guy with a Bus for sale. He said he got your name off a notice board at a garage."

"Yeah, I put one up at Eric's Bug Stop."

"This is his story: he's trying to make a flight to Hawaii tomorrow but his wallet got stolen at the airport and he owes $500 on the ticket."

"Uh huh," he said, an edge of suspicion creeping into his voice. "Is it a split-window?"

"He said it's a '66."

"Good."

"With new tires, a roof rack, and he was going on about how he had just spent $400 on a new alternator." She looked at him with the sort of bemused smile a wife has for a husband who's about to do something stupid, but not dangerous like getting a mistress or taking up skydiving.

"He's hanging around outside Continental Motors on 4th. He says he tried to sell it to them for $700, and he claims they would've taken it for reselling except they've got no room on their lot. He also says he'll take $500 for it."

"Sounds desperate. Maybe he's being pursued by drug dealers."

"Who knows? Actually," she remarked, "he sounded credible. But you can always just walk away. He called from a pay phone, and I told him that if I was able to get in touch with you, I thought you could get there about 6."

By the time I get there, all the insurance agents will be closed. I won't know whether it's stolen or has a lien on it. All the old auto-savvy, the things he had buried in his mind from 20 years ago, began to come back.

"No mechanic's going to put a lien on an old Bus," she continued. And nobody's going to owe money on it." She paused. "Anyway, if it looks good it might be worth the risk. Five hundred?" she laughed. "You were contemplating dropping four big ones! His name's René, by the way. French-Canadian, sounds like."

Continental's lot was filled with imports, everything from Mercedes to BMW to modern, sporty VWs. The only Bus was a camperized Westfalia Vanagon. A couple of mechanics stood talking with a worried-looking customer while a third one, bent over with his head under the hood, read the entrails of a Mercedes.

Just past the lane, parked against the curb, was an old, red-and-white VW Kombi Bus. With the camber of the road and the gutter along the curb, it looked like it was leaning against the curb having a rest. Dust was caked up its back and around its sides. On the back, partly obscured by the dust, was a stick-on sunburst, the granddaughter of flower power. On the roof was a homemade wooden rack, empty except for a red plastic gas can strapped on with bungee cords. There was no one in it or standing by it.

He parked nearby and walked back along the sidewalk toward it. Through the passenger-side window he could see a classic travelers mess. Rags, scraps of paper towel, empty 7-11 Slurpee cups, partly crushed plastic cola bottles, and butts from an overflowing ashtray covered the floor. The driver and passenger seats were completely wrecked, the vinyl upholstery worn through in many spots but seemingly held together by the steel springs of the seat, which could be glimpsed through the gaps.

A brown, fibrous thatch, probably the padding from the seats, was scattered around like straw on a barn floor. The rubber covering on the brake and clutch pedals was completely worn away. On the dashboard, a large speaker with its grill removed was angled toward the driver and held down by duct tape.

Moving a few steps toward the rear, he tried looking through the side windows but they were tinted purple and partly blocked off by some Indian-print fabric looped over springy plastic-coated wire, just like the curtains on Kevin's van. Maybe they attended the same sewing class? In fact, the interior looked just like Kevin's: on the floor, a mess of clothes, boots, tools and parts scattered around a couple of Rubbermaid organizers. On the fold-down bed, a tattered sleeping bag and some rumpled blankets lay in a heap. Another campsite on wheels, he thought.

"You are innerested in de Bus?" I heard in rapid-fire, French-accented English.

"Yeah, sure. You're René?"

"Very please to meet you," he said formally.

With his close-cropped hair and unshaven face he looked not unlike the Bus junkies at the show, but shabby and road-worn. Rather sharp-featured, with a ferret-like keenness of gaze, he examined the older man quickly. On his torso he wore only a curious sleeveless vest, patterned in a sort of Value Village brocade like a bizarre waistcoat; its large armholes gave a clear view of his matted armpit hair and the blue veins on his thin, hairy chest. Trying not to be obvious, the older man glanced down his arms but could see no needle tracks or razor scars. He wore a braided wrist band, the kind you learned to make in Hippie 101, to which a watch might have been attached had he needed to know the time. He wore baggy shorts, khaki-colored except where stained with dirt and age, below which extended a pair of knobby knees, bony ankles and sandals.

"Your wife tol you my story...?" he asked.

"Well, sort of... she said your wallet was stolen."

"I was at de airport, jus about to get my ticket, an was putting my tings into anudder bag. I turn my back for jus a minud an my wallet is gone."

"And you don't…"

"No, no, it was all my monay. An my ticket is jus good for tomorrow. If I can get no monay for de balance den I doan go to Hawaii." His voice trailed off. There was a pause, indecision hanging in the air. "Look, you want a Bus? Dis a good one. I jus drive here from tree-planting all summer an living in it."

The tree-planters were one of the subcultures who used old Buses like badges. They lived in their gypsy camps on the edges of clearcuts, worked hard and partied harder through the seasons when there wasn't snow in the high valleys. Then it was Mexico or, it seemed, Hawaii, until the planting season began again.

The older man looked quickly into the engine compartment, noting the remains of a nylon stocking which had once done emergency service as a fan belt. The engine started quickly, but when he tried to engage first gear it ground terribly.

"De clutch is way down on de floor," René said. "It is just de way it is now."

As a distraction, René flicked the radio on and turned the volume up. Boom! Crash! went some guitars and drums, drowning out the engine noise. "You see, de radio works!" he exclaimed happily. The older man turned it off so he could listen to this strange beast of burden.

He managed to get it rolling and away from the curb. The thing needed a clutch adjustment really badly—had he actually driven it for all these weeks and months with the clutch like this? Out in the country you wouldn't notice it so much, but in the city, it was murder. Some road testing in the madness of the rush hour traffic, it was all but impossible to do anything other than avoid running into other cars. But after a few blocks, it seemed that all the important bits, especially the brakes, worked. Not great, but they worked. Finally he got it back to the spot in front of Continental and parked and pulled on the handbrake. It almost came off in his hand. Another adjustment, at least. But did he want it? What would he do with it?

He wondered whether himself of 20 years ago, a relatively cagey and astute person used to buying and selling, scrabbling and surviving, would be laughing at the current one. His indecision was all about ego, only very little about the money. "What's five hundred bucks? It's an adventure!" he thought. Suddenly, the decision became really easy. He wouldn't, after all, have any hesitation over spending $500 on a little weekend vacation, so why should he sweat this?

After that epiphany, he caved in. They drove to a nearby bank which had a cash machine. René quietly packed his gear while he went inside and got the money. When he returned, René had all his essential gear stuffed into a single haversack and was cleaning up the mess in the interior and putting it into one of the Rubbermaid containers. A couple of dirty pots emerged from under the mess and were tossed in, followed by a propane lantern, its' base broken and glass cracked. Out of one recess he pulled a bag of cheap spanners and screwdrivers and made a point of saying they could go with the Bus, as a bonus, then threw a Chilton's service manual into it. It looked like René would never get to the bottom of his midden, as the deeper he dug the more he slowed, eventually becoming almost dreamlike as he sifted through the rubble of his recent life. He held up a grubby fork, turned it in his hand to catch the light, then with a slight shrug tossed it into the Rubbermaid. On a pad of foolscap he had written a letter, probably to a love left behind in Montréal. *Cher Sylvie*, it began. He tossed it into the Rubbermaid on top of the fork.

"Don't you want this?" the older man asked, fishing it out.

"Non. It is all past."

Next came a ten-pound bag of Basmati rice. "Dis is very good rice," René remarked, looking him directly in the eye for the first time. "You will use dis?" he asked with a cocked eyebrow.

René put his haversack and sleeping bag on a bench on the sidewalk in front of the bank, and asked indifferently whether the contents of the Rubbermaid could be dumped into a garbage can somewhere. They exchanged the money, all in 20s from the bank machine, and shook hands. As the older man drove away, leaving René with his haversack on a sidewalk bench, he tried to recall whether he had ever been that conclusive in ending one period of his life before moving onto another? René could have put some of the stuff into a cardboard box and mailed it home. Guess he didn't have a home, and just wanted to turn the page on his old life.

The following morning in the clear light of a new day the man walked out of his house to have a look at his new toy. All it lacked was a bumper sticker stating *Katmandu or Bust*. On the inside of the Bus cargo door was a Bob Marley decal, code for Dope Smoked Here. Painted on the ceiling girder at the back and visible from the bed was a frieze of little sperm-people cavorting around the words love and freedom.

With a couple of wrenches and some God-In-A-Can (a.k.a. WD-40), he crawled under the Bus back end until he could see, on the transmission housing above the rear axle on the left side, the lever that activated the clutch. The old Volksie clutch was such simple technology: with your left foot, you pushed on the pedal, which pulled a cable which pulled the lever which moved the plate away from the flywheel. No hydraulics, no computers, no mysteries. A few turns and the clutch was adjusted.

With a knife, he cut away the remains of the nylon stocking that had served as an emergency fan belt, and wondered whether it was Sylvie's. Had she left René for another, a more handsome man with a better Bus? Or had he asked her to come with him to plant trees and live in the Bus on the edge of the wilderness and she had said "No, I can't leave my job and I have to stay home and look after my mother but you can have one of my stockings as a keepsake?" There was a bit of an oil leak along the valve cover gaskets, so he made a mental note to replace them before setting off to do any serious traveling.

"A couple of weeks, maybe, and I could try a road trip?" he told himself.

On the Road Again

The Bus was fixed, tuned, cleaned and ready to go. The man knew he was risking ridicule from his friends if he set off for California to retrace his route of 25 years earlier. Maybe he needed a new set of friends. Maybe he was completely out of synch with the world around him. Maybe he had to make a trip in the slow lane and spend minimum time on the Interstates and maximum time along the little roads of William Least Heat

Moons' *Blue Highways*, tracing the coastlines of Washington, Oregon and northern California.

He realized that the Bus windshield was a two-way lens. Looking out from his slow-moving burro, he could see the fast-paced, modern world speeding by him, the occupants of the sleek modern sedans and fortress-like SUVs isolated by their wealth. Ironically, the lens worked both ways and he found that strangers were defining him through their perception of the old Bus. As he chugged around, louts flashed peace symbols and gas jockeys asked whether he'd heard that Jerry Garcia had died. He was aware of the Winnebago warriors, most of them elderly, who had the spirit of wanderlust he had when he was young. He told himself it's only because they never went further than their hair-dryer cords could reach when they were young, that's why they're on the road now. But in their RVs they're not really traveling because they're pulling along enough stuff to fill a standard bungalow. They congregated in ghettos with hook-ups and sani-dumps where they watched their TVs and whiled away the time between meals. But the question nagged at him: were they really losers or were they merely more prosperous versions of what he once was? If he went with the Bus into an RV park, would they shun him and not invite him inside their motor homes to see their gun collections and hear about their operations?

In his experience, people headed either south or west if they were looking for something. He packed in his sleeping bag, the old Coleman stove, a pot and a fry pan, and a cooler with a little food, and headed south. Once on the road he quickly fell into the routine of the smell, the noise of the engine, the Bus following ruts in the pavement like a dog following a scent. The sun poured through the windshield onto his forearm and hand. Occasionally the Bus seemed to become unhinged and wander for a minute, like it had a mind of its own. It was a vehicle for the Blue Highways, the secondary roads that are windy not twisty, rolling not hilly, without too many big bumps or dents. When he hit a real bump, like a railway crossing, the Bus let out a crashing din and the front end pitched, with him above it tossed like a cork on a stormy sea.

It was happiest at about 35 to 45 mph, and he was astonished at the gap between third and fourth gears and how little torque there was in fourth, how he felt he'd be passed going uphill

by loaded gravel trucks. He quickly relearned Bus Driving 101, rocketing down the hills breaking the sound barrier in order to rush up the other side. "Did I ever actually travel in these things?" he asked himself. It had been years since he had done any long-distance, or at least multi-hour-at-Bus-speed, driving.

But slowly, slowly, he got used to it. He found on smooth straight stretches that he could drive with just one hand, perhaps his left one, and rest his right elbow on the wheel with his hand at his chin, like Rodin's thinker. It seemed appropriate because there wasn't much else to do but think, except on rough roads where he needed all his concentration to keep the Bus from seeking a resting place in a ditch. He was uninterested in playing with the radio, and had no tapes to play, so he set to remembering whether his old Buses had radios. Gradually, an image rose in his mind, as lazy and blurred as smoke from a cigarette, of a rectangular cutout, a hole on either side and some vertical lines cut in the metal panel: just the space for one. But there was enough sound already, of metal, whining engine fan, throaty exhaust noise, rumble of tires.

It was all very simple, but it made him anxious. He was on a level with all the pickups and the Sport Utility Vehicles, but they were huge and aggressive beside his little hippie van, menacing like bikers in a bar, and he felt like he was strapped to the front bumper.

He stopped at a roadside bar, figuring on a beer and a burger before making some more miles. It was early in the evening and quiet. Only the crack of the balls on the pool table in the back room and some low murmurs of conversation competed with a Shania Twain concert on the monster TV. The bartender managed to be both busy with the accounts and attentive to him and the few others who were drinking there. She only had a couple of hours to go on her shift, she said, then home to sleep before an early start the next morning driving a school bus. Rural America.

Back in the Bus, driving south under the stars, the wind whistled through a crack in the body, or was it the vent window? The Bus pitched along on the bumps, the headlights barely cutting through the blackness ahead. So hard to concentrate: the shapes and shadows on the side of the road formed into distracting beasts that were still taking shape in his mind although he'd passed them by. Once in a while lights appeared in the tiny wing mirror and, even though it was a secondary road, they blew up in size like a balloon, then bobbed in and out impatiently until a straight stretch appeared and they could blast past.

He could see the road below through the little hole for the gas pedal stem. He was out there, and recalled Pirsig's *Zen and the Art of Motorcycle Maintenance:* You see things vacationing on a motorcycle in a way that is completely different from any other. In a car you're always in a compartment, and because you're used to it you don't realize that through that car window everything is just more TV. You're a passive observer and it is all moving by you boringly in a frame. On a cycle the frame is gone. You're completely in contact with it all. You're *in* the scene, not just watching it anymore, and the sense of presence is overwhelming. That concrete whizzing by five inches below your foot is the real thing, the same stuff you walk on, its right there, so blurred you can't focus on it.

So a VW Bus is somewhere very much there, he thought, your hand almost touching the windshield, your separation from the SUVs and semitrailers being just a shield of rusty metal with maybe a spare tire bolted to the front like a big hard pillow, a primitive airbag. A shield of rusty metal, the front of a VW Bus: that's what it reminded him of. A knights' shield: all it lacked was the handle on the inside.

Concentrate! The van swerved, unnervingly, and the raw taste of adrenalin instantly coated his tongue and jarred him awake. He caught a shallow breath: the harsh cool air from outside.

He felt insecure behind the wheel at night. Did he survive all those all-nighters because he was wide awake and a good driver, or just because he was lucky or there was no traffic on the road? Like Kerouac in *On The Road*, or John and Michelle and Denny and Cass crossing the country, Phillips writing *Go Where You Wanna Go* in his mind as the miles clicked by. The song began to play in his mind. Like that trip north from San Francisco to Vancouver in the winter, about 19 hours total, even though there was the ice storm in Grants...

Concentrate! He sat up straighter and peered more intently into the blackness. A car came at him and streaked past, very close to the center line.

Someone had said that a Bus is a metaphor for living your life at a slower pace, for being in control. As John Muir wrote, you just have to leave earlier. It has everything to do with being in control, and driving an old Bus is like flying a flag that says you can do it. And when you went slower, and took longer to start, your beast of burden lasted longer. That was conservation, in a manner of speaking, even though the VW was practically caveman technology even in the '60s and 70s. But by comparison with the American cars that were around at the time, the VW was economical, environmentally friendly (by being fuel efficient) and reliable.

John Muir. The best technical writer ever, perhaps? If he had lived, he could have coached the generations who have since tried to write manuals for TVs, DVRs, and Microsoft operating systems, and the world would be a saner place. Muir's *How to Keep Your Volkswagen Alive* was like a bible, a talisman. Years ago he had kept it in his Bus more because its mystical vibes might influence the engine than because he would be able to leap into action and fix something. It was magical and could be summoned to deal with all manner of devils. So different from other auto repair books, which lacked the funkiness and seemed somehow more manly but would say as their first instruction: Remove the engine. Well, how? Muir explains it.

The Bus ploughed on into the blackness. He thought more about its mechanical reality in the digital age. It didn't have a working speedometer and he couldn't imagine it needing one. He just went as fast as he could and knew he wasn't breaking any limits. And then there were the instruments, the two warning lights: a red one on the left that said the fan belt hadn't broken, and a green one on the right that said the engine hadn't yet dried out and seized. You didn't really need either one if your ears were working, if you were paying attention to the sounds of the machine. Like Robert Louis Stevenson's donkey, Modestine, on his travels through southern France.

I shall call you Modestine, he said aloud to his Bus. At night, Stevenson bedded down with the donkey tethered nearby and went to sleep listening to the sound of her grazing; he thought he should soon bed down and listen to his Bus ticking and cooling and rusting.

He felt the kick of adrenaline again. Was that a microsleep? He sat up straight, his back beginning to ache. There must be a place to pull off up ahead. An RV park, or a campground? He felt a curious sense of estrangement from everything, born of his first day on the road. Like Least Heat Moon, who took off after learning he'd lost his job, his wife had a lover, and the weather was breaking records for cold; a man who couldn't make things go right could at least go, he wrote. He could quit trying to get out of the way of life. Chuck routine. Live the real jeopardy of circumstance. It was a question of dignity.

Up ahead on the right an old neon sign glowed. He backed off the throttle and geared down to third, hoping it was some kind of campground. The sign was for a motel, but a painted board nearby, illuminated in the sickly green wash of a cobra-head mercury vapor lamp, said RVs - Hookups. A yellow incandescent lamp, blurred by the swarming of a thousand bugs, hung above the doorway to the office. It would have to do; he didn't know where he was, didn't want to just pull off and park. He thought quickly of spending the night on the roadside, but in his mind could hear banjos playing the opening chords of the theme from Deliverance.

His spot in the RV park was between two huge Winnebagos. With the Bus rear bench turned into a bed and his sleeping bag rolled out, he lay down and found he could watch the TV in the living room of the rolling castle next door. It wasn't a program he recognized and, anyway, he couldn't hear the sound. Should've made new curtains. It was hardly an auspicious beginning to a return to the road, but at least he had made it through the first day. He rolled the other way and was quickly asleep.

Artwork by the author

The Family Bus

Raffi Minasian

DAD NEVER DID ANYTHING HALFWAY. As the son of immigrant parents, he worked hard, served his country, and raised three great kids. At the heart of everything he did was a longing for adventure, a passionate engagement with life, and best of all a great story. "If your life isn't reading like a good book, start writing a different one."

It was 1959. Mom and Dad were newlyweds, and he'd just passed the bar exam in Boston. Secretly however, Dad longed for an adventure. In mid-1958 he placed an order for a Volkswagen Type 2 Kombi—the only new vehicle he would ever buy.

He'd read about the durable and efficient Beetle and Bus and was excited to be a part of something new. He chose the Kombi for its voluminous interior and began sketching ideas to convert his new vehicle into a camper suitable for sleeping, dining, and long-range driving. He mapped out every part of his vision but the destination.

Weeks later, Eisenhower signed H.R. 7999 into law, making Alaska the 49th state in the Union. And that settled it. The destination was chosen, maps were drawn, and provisions arranged. Dad and his new bride would embark to Anchorage, Alaska.

Dad spent weeks finishing the Bus, working nights, cutting marine-grade plywood by hand, fabricating folding cushions for bench seats, and building a hinged fold-away table for dining. When folded flat, the dining area slept two adults. A large blanket storage compartment and two side closets at the rear held suits and dresses. In the rear on the passenger side, Dad built a hinged wooden box with a rubber seal and compression clasp. The box was lined with galvanized steel and drafted cool air through a perforated bottom covering a bin for block ice, which drained its melted water into a plastic flask. Water drained from the low-cost icebox could be used for washing dishes or boiled for tea and coffee. With plenty of storage, an

overhead travel rack for larger goods, and a brand-new set of Continental tires, the Bus was ready.

Mom and Dad left Boston with two spares, spare fuel tanks, extra water, and two large suitcases wrapped in a tarp and strapped to the top. The 6,000+ mile trip took nearly two months including over a thousand miles on the then-gravel Alcan Highway, where 30 mph was a prudent speed. Mind you, this was 1959—long before convenience stations, cell phones, or GPS.

Just as Dad had envisioned, their adventure delivered a lifetime of family lore—questionable bridge crossings, wading through 8" of water for miles at the behest of an insistent compass needle, bouncing in the tundra pretending to be on the moon. Retold from his excited voice, these stories were quite different from Mom's perspective, particularly since she'd only recently left her home in the arid African desert at the time. She found snow and ice to be a very different world.

Shortly after arrival in Anchorage, Mom announced she was pregnant with my older sister. But they stayed, and I would arrive two years later. Our family would remain in Alaska until the summer before the Big Quake, when we departed to sunny Southern California.

By the late 1960s, Dad was working in a law firm. With the hippie movement in full swing, the VW Bus had become an anti-establishment icon. His law firm advised that he purchase a vehicle more "suitable to his status." So he left that firm and set up his own law office, true to his nature. He proudly piloted his Alaska-proven Bus in suit and tie through Bel Air, West LA, and Beverly Hills.

At age 11, Dad taught me to drive the Bus. "Life is not automatic. It's manual. You want control—take it. Don't let it take you." Tall in the seat and mercifully underpowered, I could operate the Bus easily without Dad moaning too much when I missed a shift or ground a gear. "Let's go get some donuts," he'd say after a driving lesson. "You get plain. You've glazed the clutch enough for a dozen donuts."

One morning in the late 1970s, Dad awakened to find the Bus had been stolen. He didn't miss a beat. We drove to the Santa

Monica police station and filed a report. They assured us it was already on the way to Mexico. Dad would have none of that. He dropped me at school and spent the rest of the day combing the streets of Venice, certain he would find a hippie driving it. Sure enough, he found it. He ran to a payphone, called the police, and waited. As the thief exited the building and walked to the Bus, Dad intervened, blocking the door. A heated exchange ensued. As Dad told the story, moments later he felt his legs get weak as the officer approached, gun drawn, yelling to get down on the ground. He hit the pavement along-side the thief. It took a moment for the police to determine who was the real owner. When he brought the Bus home, Mom said it smelled like a smokey horse barn. We aired it out for days. Sunroof fully open, baking soda sprinkled on surfaces. Dad refused to press charges on one condition; he invited the thief to the house and insisted he help clean the Bus.

In 1985, Dad passed away. My sister and brother and I had all enjoyed many memorable days camping with the VW, and we'd all learned to drive on it, but it had lost its most significant part. Without Dad, the family Bus no longer had the right driver. My younger brother became the caretaker. As much as he enjoyed it, after six years, he didn't have a place for it in his life. We rebuilt the engine and took it to the Pomona swap meet. It sold in a matter of days.

Then, in 2012, I posted an inquiry on TheSamba.com. Like Bring-a-Trailer, the Samba community did not let me down (https://www.thesamba.com/vw/forum/viewtopic.php?t=499274&postdays=0&postorder=asc&start=0)

Within a few days people were reflecting on the rarity of our Bus, and tapping their memory banks for its whereabouts. Eventually it was revealed that it had been sold to a fellow in the Netherlands in the 1990s. The owner emerged, posting pictures of our family Bus still wearing the factory blue paint.

The damaged rear quarter panel, which Dad had insisted was the handiwork of an angry bull moose in 1961 (a story he relished telling while showing off the dents), was finally repaired. But underneath the hippie-style floral motif, the rest of the Bus remained largely original.

Sadly, Dad's entire custom interior was long gone—replaced with standard VW seats. This Dutch owner had since sold it on, but said it remained in much the same condition. Ten years later, it's likely still unchanged (I like to think), a lasting relic of family adventure, now a collector's item.

I often think about our old Bus, not just because I see variants selling for $100k today and shake my head at getting $4k for it. Rather, it's because our Bus was the keeper of our family's adventures. It taught me how to appreciate cars and embodied the sense of daring and possibility that Mom and Dad embraced as a young couple, bravely homesteading in a unique and wild part of the world. Its eleven windows provided me with a view on my own life—staring at stars through the panoramic sunroof, gazing out the back window as the past recedes, or facing the road ahead through split windshield panes. Once chosen for its roomy interior, my father's old VW Bus now contains much more—my connection to my father, the experiences that shaped my own vision for my own future, a philosophy of shifting one's own gears on the road of life, and above all the value of a great story.

This story first published January 22, 2022, Bringatrailer.com.

VW Busing Today

Finding a Bus

Kombi at the Crossroads

Tom Forhan

BACK IN THE SIXTIES, Bert Roan bought his 1959 Kombi for deer hunting. It still helps him fill the freezer today, though things have changed a bit… but I am getting a little ahead of the story.

I'd first seen the Kombi while bicycling along a wooded country road. It was an archetypal find, sitting among some scrub and vines, behind a metal-clad pole barn and a faded pink and white trailer. Out in front, a stocky man with dark gray hair was tending a small, smoky fire built inside an old truck tire rim.

I left my bike by the road, walked back, and introduced myself. I offered pleasantries, and I told him I had an old VW Bus and had noticed his.

Summarily, he looked up. "It's not for sale."

"Oh," I said. "I'm out here on vacation, nowhere near home. Got one kind of like it; I just wanted to take a look."

He poked at the fire a bit. "People don't stop here often, but the only reason they do is 'cause of that Bus. Years ago, a hippie parked his old VW Bus on the road, and walked up the drive with a bag of tools on his shoulder. Told me he needed the generator. Didn't ask, didn't offer to pay, just said he needed it to get back home. I told him to go to hell.

"Last year someone just helped themselves. Messed up the dashboard, took that VW thing off the front. Really made me mad, since when I drove it back and parked it there, everything was there and everything worked."

"So it was running when you parked it. When was that?" I asked.

"Well, I bought it for deer hunting. That ground clearance and traction were great on the sandy two-track roads around here. But then the government started buying up all the hunting lands for the park. Closed all the trails, so I changed my plans. Musta been around 1975 when I stopped driving it.

"Lately, my wife's health has been kind of poor; we only get up here weekends now, and not every one at that. We bought this place in 1950; still try to get here when we can. Since folks have been messing with that Bus, I like to walk back and check on it each time I visit."

Straightening out of his crouch, he said, "Let's go have a look."

We walked around the back of the barn. My first good look was from the rear, and I saw original (and desirable) round taillights and a rectangular rear window. Not ancient, but a respectable age. The body was the lovely Dove Blue, but worried with lots of surface rust, especially on the roof. A long time ago, someone had made a quick job of repairing the rockers with galvanized sheet metal. "With all the problems you're having, why don't you take those taillights off and stop tempting people?" I asked.

Bert did not want to talk about parts. He pointed up the hill to the right. "There are two deer runs there, one coming down each side, then they join up and pass us over there, twenty feet from the cargo door. On the other side, deer come into the pasture from the south, walk along the edge, and then move across in front of the Bus. So there are three natural deer runs on my property, and that's why I parked it here. It's right at the crossroads! Of course, they've been walking past the Bus all year, and it's only in late November when I'm sitting out here," he chuckled.

He focused on the Kombi again, and opened up the engine lid. It looked like the proper 36 horsepower engine, #2646017, with the cast-in generator stand and funky squashed fuel pump. A six-volt battery to the right, daylight visible below it, held up only by the battery cables. To the left was an Eberspacher gasoline heater.

I took a close look at the heater. He whispered conspiratorially, "That heater is what makes the whole thing work. I charge up the battery, put some fuel in the tank each fall, and I have my own heated deer blind!"

"It still runs?" I asked, trying not to sound overly amazed.

"Yeah, sure. The heater, anyway. I bring out a big pot of goulash, too, put it under the rear seat by the heat outlet, and that damn heater warms me up, inside and out!"

At this point, he lifted the rear hatch. A mass of insulation, seeds, mouse dung, and other assorted detritus fell out. There was strong aroma of musk and urine. "The rest of the year the raccoons call it home," guessed Bert. "I don't mind it much in hunting season. The cold keeps the smell down." I looked beyond the accumulation. The radio cover plate looked pristine, and the dome light lens was intact and perfect.

That was about all the good parts.

Bert moved around to the passenger side, and showed me how he had carefully greased the hinges over the years. The cargo doors opened beautifully.

Inside, a three-passenger middle seat faced the rear, and a small makeshift table sat between the two. The seat color was strange, a light yellow green. "Those aren't the originals. The seats that came with it were shot and I got these off a guy who was making his Bus into a dune buggy or some such thing."

"Those middle seats are hard to find," I said. "Everybody took them out and threw them away. A three-passenger seat like this is what I need for my project..." But he didn't rise to the bait.

Next, we moved up to the front and he opened the passenger door. I reached in and lifted up the seat back. "Yes, it still has the spare," said Bert. But I was looking for the production plate, and I found it:

13 11 8
372 13 175
UF 231 BLUE 409913

I majored in anthropology in college, even did some graduate work. I had wanted to decipher the Mayan hieroglyphs. I would imagine myself at an archeological site in the Yucatan, walking up to a fallen stele, just unearthed from the humus of the jungle floor. The carving, not having seen the light of day for twelve centuries, would be surrounded by a cluster of scholars and Mayan workers, anxious to hear the words of the ancients. I would consider the inscription, decode the words and numbers and finally make a pronouncement. Something like: "On June 8, 756, the Butterfly Lord ascended the throne, celebrating the passing of his mother, the Lady Ix Chel."

Instead, I found myself with yet another Splitty moldering away in the back woods, and I was doing the decoding for Bert Roan:

"Built November 13, 1958."

"That guy who sold it to me ripped me off—he said it was a 1959!"

"Well, November would put it in the 1959 model year. 372—that's a bit of an unknown, probably US export equipment. 13—middle and rear seat, and 175 refers to the bumper overriders. UF: we know U is a USA designation, but the scholars are still working on the meaning of whatever letter follows the U. 231—that means it's a Kombi model. BLUE is the color, or course, Dove Blue, I think it was called."

"Cripes," said Bert. "I mean it's pretty obvious it's blue, right? Why would they stamp it on a damn plate?"

I let that one go by. "…and the last number is the vehicle serial number." I retreated from the front seat, noting that the steering wheel—black, of course—had no apparent cracks.

We moved around to the front. It was clear that the VW emblem had been removed in the not too distant past, the paint underneath still clean and bright. I took a picture of Bert and his Bus.

As we walked back to the trailer, Bert appeared pensive. Reconsidering the issue of the middle seat perhaps? My hopes were quickly dashed.

"You know," he said thoughtfully, "if I would just smash those taillights, I'll bet no one would ever bother my Bus again."

Truth & Beauty

Rick MacCornack

I HAVE ENJOYED READING THE STORIES of others about something which most people find absurd. Getting excited about an old, underpowered, unsafe-at-any-speed, boxy vehicle which typically developed cancer at an early age seems like an oxymoron to most folks. Yet I was pleased and amazed to find out that there is still life out there—true, blood-rushing enthusiasm rooted as much in an idea as an object. After 20-odd years of being anesthetized by various marques of Swedish and Japanese descent, I woke up, not with a jolt, but with a gradual revelation and reintroduction to a truth I once took for granted. Here's how it happened to me.

Two years ago we moved to a gorgeous island in the Pacific Northwest, a major change of pace from a series of urban-based moves. It took us back in time physically and mentally to a less-rushed, self-conscious and self-justifying era. And with the move came the steady rush of self-discovery which seems to occur when you stop, look and listen to the world around you. Other things happened. The network of casual conversations in ferry lines led to a re-awakening of an earlier time, a connection to a period in my life when progress was measured by ideals, not fiscal pressure. One day, a fellow commuter began talking about friends of his on the island who had a VW Bus for sale. I was curious enough to take a look. It turned out to be a 1973 pseudo camper, of no interest to me. But deep in the dust-covered shed that sat nearby under tall pines was the back end of an older dusty red and white Bus. Closer inspection revealed that it was a Deluxe 21-window '67, complete and straight as an arrow. Adrenalin started rushing at a rate that surprised me. It was hard to believe. Underneath the accumulated grime was an almost rust and dent-free vehicle that had survived the ebb and flow of the last 25 years totally unscathed. Everything worked, even the Sapphire III AM radio and the windshield washer. The last Bus I had owned had been a '66 Standard in the same color scheme. That was 22 years ago. Memory flashes haunted me. I was excited, but the owner was ambivalent about letting go of a family treasure. Then my middle-aged, practical, safety-minded perspective on life began to beat up my enthusiasm, but not for long.

After several weeks had passed, I called the owner's wife. She was clearly the person who had to be convinced that this Bus would be happier in my garage than in her shed. Her story unfolded: The Bus had belonged to her husband's father, who bought it new in Lompoc, California in November, 1967. He had been a Boeing engineer and had driven and cared for it as one would expect an engineer to do. When he died in 1980, his son inherited it. He drove it around the island for several years and loved it as his father had. During the son's tenure, the original engine got a rebuild two-thirds of the way to the century mark and then died at 100,116. Into the shed it went. Not long after, the son purchased a duplicate parts Bus in blue and white, a Bus that was held together by rust. Its purpose was to provide a few minor goodies in a long-term dream to restore the red Bus. Then dreams got distant. That's when I got close. Realizing the emotional ties which had developed over the years with this one-family treasure, I was prepared to go to the wall. Having been in their position myself, I knew what I was up against. I made an extremely attractive offer for both Buses and promised them the red Bus would never move off the island. They were more interested in the commitment than the price offer. The red Bus was in my garage that afternoon with visiting rights guaranteed. The blue Bus made its way to the mainland, where its new owner discovered, after a false start, that the volume of rust was not worth the effort. We recently found out that the blue Bus had once belonged to a friend of ours. She had driven it out from Michigan in the 1970's, explaining the volume of rust. When the highway became too noticeable under her feet, she sold it for parts. Small world, the Bus world.

With the red Bus now in hand, I had to make a decision. Would it be realistic to give up the creature comforts and reliability of our modern car? Being a three-car family seemed out of the question since one would have to live outdoors (my wife is the second owner of a nearly showroom condition '66 sedan named Cheena Bug). Was I nuts to even think of using the Bus as a daily driver? Would it make financial sense? Would it be practical? Months slipped by as I spent weekends poking around my new find. In the dead of winter, the answer came to me: I started listening to times past. I realized I had already begun thinking about this new friend in terms of a name.

Old Arlo had a voice that came alive for me. He was a presence, a tie, not just to my own experiences through the late '60's and early '70's, but to a moment in time when it was easy to be in touch with the road, actually and figuratively. Today, our family is changed by the presence of this old friend. We discover daily the joys of practical transport and functional design. Seats fit people of all sizes. There are some basic truths: nothing holds more than a box; greenhouses let in light. For years I had slipped into thinking that cars had improved through CAD-designed, ergonomically-oriented engineering. Yes, but I rediscovered that there's no match for the thrill of being in the cab, lounging comfortably on the wheel, peering down on the road ahead through split windows with sun streaming in from all directions, including the yawning hole in the rolled back rag top. My son, who is seven, had never known that riding in a vehicle could be so much fun. My daughter is too young to comment, but she knows that winter time means she rides with blankets. We are all amused by the attention we get. The number of people who ask us at stop lights, "Do you want to sell it," almost gets tiring. We are known by the vehicle we drive.

The speeding ticket we got this morning... well, a few things have changed underneath to which I haven't accommodated. I wanted to keep the Bus completely stock on the upside. I also wanted to have a daily driver to replace our Japanese wagon, a hard act to follow, mechanically-speaking. So, I sat down with our fanatic mechanic and designed the ideal road Bus for us. We ended up with an 1800cc blueprinted and balanced dual port with a double barrel Weber and tuned free-flow exhaust. This was hitched to a beefy transaxle with taller 3rd and 4th gears. KYB gas shocks, front and rear sway bars and a complete brake rebuild finished the mechanical work. For an old VW Bus, it moves with the pack. We've reduced gust-driven automatic lane changes from three to one. We accelerate up hills in fourth. And best of all, it still sounds like a Bus.

Our life is different now. Commuting is an experience, not a chore. I feel alive, in touch with the elements, and sometimes I am. And now we discover there's more folks like us out there—lots more. All over the place. That's a rush that replaces all those years of driving in a soundproof box, out of touch, out of tune. Old Arlo has brought us back on the path again, reminding us—sometimes relentlessly—that life is at its best when it is lived from the soul.

Postscript

Thirteen years have passed since this story was written. Much has happened in a world which has become highly technologically evolved in ways which are not all good for its inhabitants. In a new millennium, we have to work hard to balance what is good, true and meaningful in our lives. This is not to romanticize the past, which most of us tend to do as we get older. Times change and the lenses through which we view and interpret the world change as well. But some basic truths that define quality beyond the moment and the individual carry on. In its design, the Microbus was purposeful. It could carry more than it should have. It created pleasure and value from its utility for those who could accommodate its design limitations. It was a perfect machine that was beautiful because of its functionality. It was also unsafe unless handled purposefully and with an intuitive sense of physics. It was certainly underpowered, requiring creativity and forethought in planning one's route. All of these qualities contributed to its icon status, a vehicle that was so eccentric in its place alongside the majority of vehicles of its time that it rose above the crowd as decades passed.

In 1992 my 1967 Deluxe Microbus fit perfectly into our life as sole transportation. Thirteen years later it is hard to admit that, over the years, I succumbed to pressures of growing kids and a demanding profession. Freeway driving became increasingly risky with increasing speed and danger posed by well-insulated, over powered vehicles driven by latte-drinking, cell phone clutching idiots. Too many life-threatening close calls with kids in the back put an unnatural fear in this driver. It created a huge personal conflict. Since my life has never included a big garage, I could not rationalize keeping my Bus under a tarp in the wet Northwest climate. Cold storage was out of the question with college educations looming. I was confronted with choosing between emotions and logic. One grey morning in December as I was shifting my way to work on the mainland, a man came running after me (literally) with an attractive offer. Arlo now resides in a dry garage not far from our island, completely restored. That knowledge has been the only good justification for my decision to sell. Some day, when our kids are out of college, my one remaining air-cooled (a 1963 Karmann Ghia convertible which has been sitting in the back of a body shop for 10 years!) will be completed and sold for—you guessed it—a restored 1967 Deluxe Microbus. I might even get lucky and find Arlo ready to come back home. If it happens, he will be confined to island transport on back roads where the speed limit is still commensurate with his design.

Daily Driver Delusions

Everett Barnes

IT ALL STARTED ON A SATURDAY. I had decided to look for a Bus to use as a daily driver and was perusing the local Auto Trader classifieds when I saw it:

> *"1958 Bus, Kombi model, 7 doors, sunroof, all original, complete, needs paint, lowered, $2000."*

Whoa! A '58 Double Door Kombi?!? It was all a daze as the phone seemed to spring into my hands and dial itself. The owner's mother answered the phone and indicated her son was not home but he would call me back when he returned.

A few hours later, I got the return call. He began with what seemed like a prepared speech: "It's a '58 Kombi. All the parts are there. It has been primered with the good stuff and is almost ready for paint. The only body work it needs is a little bit of welding on the passenger front floor, the windshield was leaking when I bought it and there are a few holes. Right now it is at a local shop. I took it there because it was overheating and he repaired it. I had some money trouble and could not pay for the repairs. Now I need to sell it because I owe the shop over $1000 for repairs and 3 months of storage fees. The $2000 price is firm."

"Does it have all the seats?" I asked.

"The front seat is there. There are no rear seats."

"Well, maybe it didn't come with rear seats…" I mumbled under my breath, then replied "Okay, I would like to come see it. Can I get the VIN number?"

He was quick on the reply. "I don't have the pink slip in front of me but the number of the shop is KL5-3346. They know I am selling it and can give you more information about it and any work they did. I'll try and find the pink slip in the meantime."

"The Bus is in your name, right?"

"Oh yeah, I've owned it for about a year, just haven't driven it much."

"Okay, I'll call them. When can I come see it?"

"I have to go out for the rest of the day, call me tomorrow and I can meet you at the shop."

I called the shop, they were closed.

Sunday

I woke up early, excited to go see the Bus as early as possible. My wife, Jen, convinced me that I should wait until at least 9:00 a.m. to call, so I did. I got his machine and left a message, then continued trying to call him at various intervals throughout the day with no luck. Finally, I got a call back late that evening that he had dug up the pink slip. I retrieved the VIN information and consulted my reference books. Damn, it's a '63! I really wanted a split-case era Bus, but man, a complete and original Double Door Kombi? I had to at least see it!

"Can I come see it today?" I asked.

"No, I found out the shop is closed today. Call me tomorrow and we can meet over there after work."

"Okay."

By this time, I've decided I want the vehicle. A complete '63 Double Door Kombi in excellent shape for around $2000? Sounds like a deal!

Called the guy multiple times Monday and Tuesday, always got the message machine, which was full. My mind was racing. *Is the machine full of potential buyers? Is the Bus sold already? Why isn't he calling me back?*

Wednesday

Because of my inability to contact the owner, I decide to call the shop to see what information they have on the vehicle.

"Hello, I'm calling about the Bus stored at your shop that's for sale," I began.

"My Bus? I want $1500 for it."

"Oh, I thought it was just in storage at your shop, waiting for the owner to pay his bill."

"No, it's mine, I'm submitting the paperwork today to get it put into my name, and I've had a lien on the vehicle for three months. The owner is in jail in San Jose anyway," he replied, as if that was a common occurrence.

Now I was getting frustrated. What the heck was going on? Had he been in jail the last few days? That's why I haven't heard from him? Okay, calm down, typical thing that would happen to me now that I'm seriously interested in the Bus. Just play along…

"Oh, really? Well, I am interested in it. When will it be in your name?"

"I'm going to the DMV tomorrow."

"I would like to come see it this weekend."

"Call me Saturday morning and you can come out."

Now I'm just nervous. Does the seller even own the Bus? Well, I have the VIN number. I call the Department of Motor Vehicles to see if he is the registered owner. They were polite but informed me they could not give me that information. Fine, I'll call the police station.

"Hello, I am interested in purchasing a vehicle I have found and wish to verify the ownership of it."

"Why would you need to do that?"

"Well, the supposed owner may be in jail right now so I just thought I would check."

"Go ahead."

I relayed the ownership information to the police and they verified he was still the owner, at least for now. I then decided to call the San Jose jail to check his release date. You'd think the information might be private but no, they came right out and tell me he's not getting out, the charge is fraud and with his priors, he is being held until his arraignment. Well, maybe the shop owner's lien will go through and I can just buy it from him.

Thursday

The owner calls me back! Says he was just off visiting his friend for a few days and couldn't get back to me. Uh-huh, either that or you were in JAIL! It's getting pretty obvious that fraud is in his veins but I'm determined that I have got to see the Bus, if only to have a complete story about it. I tell him I'm going to see it on Saturday at the shop and ask him again if he has a pink slip in his name.

"Yes, I have it right in front of me. Just call me after you go see it and make me an offer. I've got to sell it ASAP so make me an offer."

Righhhht, now he's just trying to rip somebody off when he knows he's losing ownership of the vehicle. I decide to call the jail again, to make sure he didn't escape or something, to see if he had a bench warrant out for his arrest, and to find out why he was he even let out. Maybe I got his name wrong… I call the San Jose jail again to see when he's getting out.

"Oh, it looks like we let him out on his own recognizance. We needed room for a bunch of drunks and DUIs we arrested Wednesday night. His court date is in two weeks." What? Nice legal system we have here, they let out someone with multiple counts of fraud to let some drunks sleep it off?

Saturday

I wake up early again, ready to go see the Bus. I'm a little distraught at the circumstances and am wondering if this is just a big waste of time. I set up the time to go over there and call my brother, relating to him the story so far. He decides to come with me, if only to see what should be a nice Bus. Jen, Dave, and I pile into Jen's car and make the one-hour drive across the Bay to his shop.

We arrived at what looked like a normal repair shop, big drive-through double doors in front, six bays inside, all with various vehicles up on lifts having work performed. A medium-height, medium-build sleazy-looking man seemed to be supervising one of the vehicles. That must be the guy. I walked over.

"Hi! I'm Everett, here about the Bus."

"It's out back, go through there. The keys are in it." He points out through the back double bay doors of his repair shop. As we walk outside, I ready myself for the inspection. My hopes were up. I guess they shouldn't have been by this point but I was still clinging to the belief that the seller wasn't that bad, and the Bus would make up for all the hassle I had to go through to get it. There it sat, squeezed in between an old MG and a crappy Olds that had obviously been in a fatal accident. The gray primer looked fairly new, and the body appeared straight, at least the upper half. I walked up the side to the cab for a look at the interior. This is it? You call this all original? Black vinyl interior panels dumped into the walk-through partition? Highback seats grafted in from who knows what, obviously not any sort of VW. What sort of radio requires you to cut a hole that big in the dash? Okay, calm down, the body looks straight. Check the passenger side floor. Damn! I wouldn't describe that nightmare under the passenger side of the front floor mat as a few holes to be welded up, more like a few pieces of metal are left holding the floor intact! I'm not even sure a passenger could put their feet down without going through the floor! Is that rust at the bottom of the cargo doors? I bend down for a closer look. Are the rockers supposed to look wavy? I prod a little with my finger and a piece falls inward. Oh man, talk about your serious Bondo job… Well, it runs nice, right? Let's check out the engine. Yes, I see why it could be overheating, there are no heater hoses coming off the fan shroud and no engine seals in sight. What exactly did the repair shop fix for that $1000?

Well, maybe I can talk the guy down once I explain all the stuff that is wrong with it. I may as well drive it, what else could be wrong? After much maneuvering and Jen and Dave flashing various hand signals, I get the Bus out from the back of his shop and into the interior of the repair bay. Sure doesn't feel like a stock engine but maybe I'm confused by the 1700 lb. pressure plate and the fact that it has Type 3 axles and no reduction boxes. I get it through the repair bay and out to the front entrance to the shop, scraping the dual quiet pack exhaust on everything possible along the way. It does seem like the engine has a lot of power, even at low rpms. Maybe it's a 1776cc—it did have some funky Weber carb on it. Doesn't look like there's much chance I will be buying it so might as well have a little fun. I rev the engine up and drop the clutch as I exit his shop, spinning the rear tires and sliding into a right-hand turn going south. Whoa, this Bus is fast! I unintentionally accelerate on the four-lane main street to 50 mph, getting a little scared as I notice the steering wheel has wayyy too much play in it to drive safely. I downshift to second on the next turn, making sure I can handle the steering, and then punch it into the straight-away, rising back up to 55 mph quickly and effortlessly. Okay, enough fun, I've gone a mile or so, better turn around and head back.

I begin to head around the block, making a right turn, then another right turn when all of a sudden, the shifter goes slack. The gear shift is in neutral and won't go back into gear! And why is the idle so high now? I pull up the shift boot to check the shifter bolts: no, they are tight, the shifter couldn't have moved. Maybe it's the shift coupler. Well, if the Bus wasn't so low, I could take a look. Forget it, I'm only about a mile away from the shop now, so I'll just park it and walk back. So I got out, went to push the Bus to the side using the door jamb. What the heck? I can't even move it! Okay, okay, brakes must be binding a little, crank the steering wheel, go to the back and really push. Damn, I can barely get it to move. Crap, there's a fire hydrant nearby, can't park it there anyway. Okay, there's a spot about 20 yards up the street. Ugh, how can the brakes be this tight?!? Did I put the e-brake on? Nope. A few passers-by notice my predicament and help me push it over to the side by the hydrant. Forget it, I'm leaving it right here, and if it gets towed, that's his problem; I'm heading back to the shop.

Meanwhile, Dave and Jen are back at the shop, wondering what happened to me. The shop owner keeps coming out to the front of his shop and looking around, checking to see if Dave and Jen are still there and making little comments under his breath. By this time, they've both decided he is a serious a**hole. Jen convinces Dave to head out in her car to look for me. He catches me walking when I'm about halfway back and we cruise back to the shop.

"Where's the Bus?"

"It broke down."

"Oh, s**t."

"My words exactly."

I enter the shop to find the guy talking on the phone. He takes his time finishing the conversation and hangs up.

"The Bus broke down," I say.

"What happened?"

"I'm not sure. The gearshift was in neutral and I couldn't put it into gear…" I begin to explain the steps I tried but he just cuts me off.

"Oh, yeah, that happened once before. I just gotta adjust the shifter cables."

"Uh, there aren't any cables."

"I've been working on cars for 20 years. YOU don't tell ME about them."

"Okayyyy." I glance at my brother and he has the same "this guy is insane" look on his face that I have on mine.

Well, I decide to see if he is now the legal owner, so maybe I can cut a deal.

"When will the Bus be legally in your name?" I ask.

"It is now," he answers as if he owned it all along.

Oh, really? I think to myself but say "Do you have the paperwork from the DMV?"

"Well, it's at my house but I'll go get it if you REALLY need to see it."

"Yes, I will, if we can arrive at a price. It seemed to run really strong before it broke down. What was your asking price again?"

"It's $1500."

"Well, that would be fair but most of the parts on it are not '63. It needs a lot of welding and bodywork. A lot of parts are missing, plus now it's not drivable. So, what's the lowest you will go?"

"Make me an offer."

"$400, since now I'll have to pay to get it towed home."

"No way, I could paint it and sell it for at least $2500. I just want it out of my shop. The owner owes me over $1000 in storage charges anyway."

I hold back a laugh and just smile. "We both know storage charges are bull. I'd pay you more if I could drive it away."

"I could fix the shifter problem," he offers.

"Okay, when would you do that?"

"Today works. My labor rate is $55/hour."

I am stunned. This guy is definitely insane.

"Oh, I thought you meant you would fix it in order to sell the Bus."

"You're not going to pay me to fix it?"

At this moment, I finally decide to give it up. Apparently, this guy thinks he's some sort of brilliant scam artist. It's apparent that no deal will be made.

"Bye."

"Wait, I thought you wanted it."

"Not for more than $400. I doubt it is even in your name. Call me if you change your mind, you have my number. Bye."

We left.

I feel sorry for his paying customers...

The Treasure Bus

Keith Price

LEAVE NO STONE UNTURNED. Follow every lead. Call about every classified ad. Old Volkswagens can show up in the strangest places, containing even stranger cargo. So it was with our "Treasure Bus."

Last August, Barb and I took the kids away to the family cottage in our 1971 Westfalia Campmobile. While visiting Big Rapids, home of Ferris State University, we spotted homemade signs on every storefront reading:

ESTATE SALE
Household Items, Sporting Goods, Tools, VW Minivan

Drawn like an electromagnet to the given address, I visualized a sealing wax red and ivory 1959 Sunroof Deluxe with a complete interior, no rust, and a smooth running 40 hp motor.

In reality, it turned out to be a white 1967 Kombi with vicious rocker panel and cargo floor rust. The estate sale ringleader assured me that the Bus, priced at $500, would run but wouldn't idle. It had 12 volt electrics and an original governor on the throttle linkage. My ever-present Idiot Book identified the engine case as a '66 1300. A quick half turn of the adjustment screw had the motor idling placidly. The clutch disengaged and the brake pedal was mushy. The Bus featured a unique homemade wooden camper interior with several storage cabinets. In Kombi tradition, only the rearmost side windows were pop-outs. Also included were some Beetle seats and a complete '60 36 hp long block, turning freely.

Thinking I could part this mess out for a small fortune, I offered $100 to "get the monkey off their backs." A family conference ensued with much mumbling and hissing. We have a deal! After I removed the ghastly foam rubber mattress from the rear and scanned the cab for clues, I found a service logbook documenting everything from delivery at Tom Sullivan VW in March of '67, through a transmission fluid change in June of '93. Every valve adjustment, oil change, brake shoe and short block was noted in painstaking accuracy with dates and recorded mileage. The odometer admitted to 71K on its second spin.

"It seems OK mechanically," I deadpanned to the family point person, a scowling woman about my age.

"My stepfather related to things, not people!" she sneered, handing me the endorsed, original owner's title.

Within 15 minutes, I had checked the oil and fan belt tension, topped off the fuel tank and inflated a low tire. We were cruising steady down US 131. The reduction boxes were quiet, the gas gauge worked and it ran like a train. Fuming, Barb had to break 70 mph in the '71 Westy to keep up with me.

Back at the cottage, I began the arduous task of body rust assessment and inventory of contents. In addition to extreme frame cancer at the rear torsion bar mounting points, we found two ladies' diamond rings, a mountain of costume jewelry, two 14k gold ladies' dress watches, some very old silver dollars and several assorted foreign coins. We also found several men's watches, lots of funky sunglasses, some tools, mosquito netting for two, some camping gear, and some slinky black lingerie with garter belts. The literature consisted of original owners and service manuals, county maps with trout streams marked with colored pencils, and the aforementioned service logbook.

Last October, I brought the Bus 170 miles home to Royal Oak. The only required fix has been a front brake line. My six-year-old son Hal and I painted the Bus in a free-form Sixties retro motif, using every spray can of Krylon, Rust-O-Leum, and BBQ paint I could find in the basement. The plan now is to get some U-channel welded to the frame rails as a Band-Aid fix. Then I'll drive it occasionally to the delight of my children, hit a few swap meets, and let it serve as a reminder to my neighbors not to take life so seriously.

Seek and ye shall find.

Bus Farming in Rhode Island

Jean-Paul Jacquet

SOME YEARS AGO, Alyce and I went on a weekend drive out from our home in Providence, R.I. It was a beautiful fall day, and we were driving our Bus—the safari windows were open, the Bus had just been washed, and we were feeling pretty good in it. We went looking for an ice cream stand, and it just so happened that at the particular ice cream stand we found there was a hot rod/custom car show going on across the street, so we pulled in.

After we checked out the cars and returned to our Bus, a few people had gathered around our Bus. One of these folks, Austin, started talking about the Bus, and the collection of Buses that his father had, an impressive number. It sounded like a crazy story but we decided to hook up with him the following week and see them.

Austin's father's house is absolutely in the middle of nowhere. We met up with Austin at a CVS pharmacy in a town called Chepachet, just west of Providence near the Connecticut border, and he escorted us to the house. We went down lots of little winding dirt roads, and ended up at a little old New England-type farmhouse.

From the driveway, first we saw one Beetle, then a Bus. But as we looked deeper into the woods, we could see that it was just full of Volkswagen Buses, and that they were all split-window Buses. We tried to contain ourselves, but we were eager to start venturing into the woods.

My guess is that there were at least 20, maybe more, out there. And they were not in that bad of a shape. Every Bus seemed to be a different model, and a lot I recognized, but it was the first time I'd seen them. Alyce, Austin, and I excitedly wandered around marveling at this amazing hidden collection of Buses.

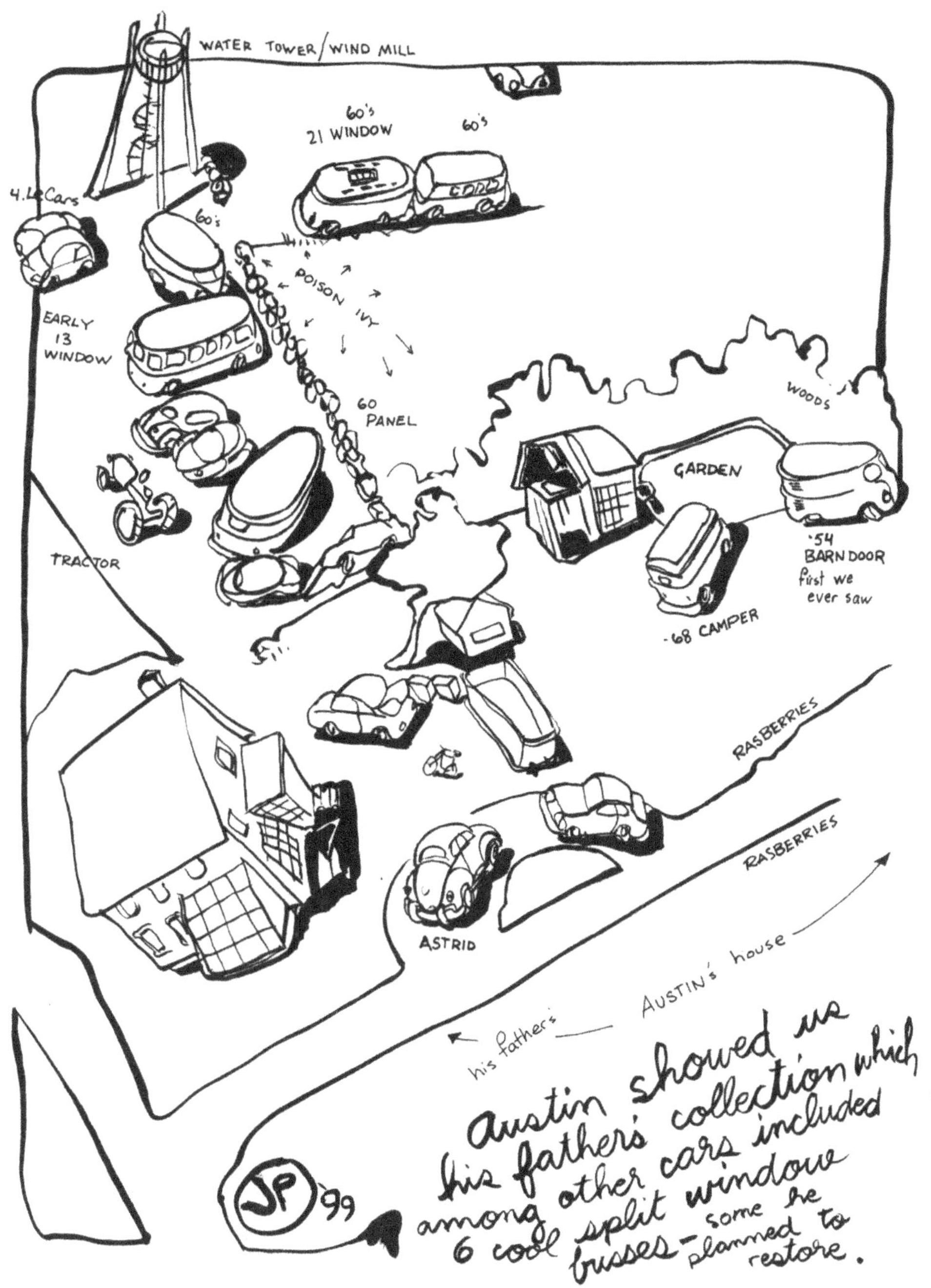

WATER TOWER / WIND MILL
60's
21 WINDOW
60's
4 L Cars
60's
EARLY
13
WINDOW
POISON IVY
60 PANEL
WOODS
GARDEN
TRACTOR
·54
BARN DOOR
first we
ever saw
·68 CAMPER
RASBERRIES
RASBERRIES
ASTRID
his father's
AUSTIN's house
JP 99
austin showed us
his father's collection which
among other cars included
6 cool split window
busses — some he
planned to
restore.

Because of a bad fuel pump...
a customer of Bills' (Engines By Benz)
managed to drive 30 miles by
creatively rigging up a hose
that ran from the gas
tank to the front of the
bus, and by blowing
into the hose he
managed to keep
the fuel tank
pressurized enough
to force gas into
the carburetor.

Imagine the lungs
on this guy...

When the fuel pump died on a family trip to Canada (in the 60's), Austin's father cut a hole above the engine compartment – attached a hose with a funnel to the carburator and had his two daughters feed fuel to the engine for the RIDE home to Rhode Island.
MOTHER, FATHER, and 6 CHILDREN in a VW bus.
JP '99

And then we finally met Austin's father—a great character. The type of guy everyone would want to have as a grandfather. He had all these knick-knacks around, all these crazy little inventions. I think in the drawing there is a windmill or a water tower he started to construct and it never quite worked, but he planned to one day complete it. He started getting into stories of when the farm was a working farm and he was using Volkswagens to transport stuff, such as a cow. That's where the drawing of the "real kicker" comes in: the cow in the back kicking him. There was also the story of their trip to Canada about 30 years ago. On their way back the fuel pump died, and his solution was to cut a little hole above the engine compartment and attach a plastic hose with a funnel to the carburetor and have two of his daughters supply fuel to the engine through this contraption for their ride home. Three or four hours of pouring gas into the engine! They made it back. That was pretty impressive!

I've been meaning to go back there, and chat some more, but I'm not sure I could find the place again. Perhaps if I wandered around for a day, I might be able to find it. Alyce and I actually got lost getting out of there—and it's kind of hard to get lost in Rhode Island. A difficult place to find!

The drawing of the guy with the big lungs is my take on a story told by Bill Benz, a great VW mechanic in Providence, Rhode Island: a guy came into his shop having driven from New Bedford, Massachusetts, which is maybe 30 to 40 minutes away, again a bad fuel pump. His solution was to put a hose into the gas tank, run it around the Bus, and keep blowing in it, thus creating pressure that would push fuel into the engine. That's one solution that I wouldn't have thought of.

VW Busing Today

Living with a Bus

My Childhood

Flash qFiasco

SO, YOU THINK YOU'VE HEARD A GOOD STORY about a mint condition VW Bus that's been parked in a garage for 30 years and hardly ever been driven? And it's for sale cheap? I'm about to tell you another one. But before I do, I have to tell you a third one. It's about my miserable childhood in Disturbia, a meaningless succession of decades filled with asphalt, TV, and small appliances. Our respite was a '64 VW Camper, pearly white. We drove it over the Rockies. We drove it across the Great Plains, over the High Sierra, through Death Valley, around Lake Tahoe, over the Golden Gate Bridge. Yes, we were intrepid campers. I loved that car and I loved the good times we had in it. But all things must pass…

Suddenly it's 30 years later. My father still drives VW Buses, newer versions and farther afield. He's thrashing around Alaska in a Syncro these days… but that would be a different story. Meanwhile, I live in Germany and have become—shudder—an adult, though I cannot for the life of me recall when it happened. No more childhood frivolities. Until…

One day, my friend Marco the Mechanic spots a VW Bus for sale, mint condition, cheap. He doesn't have the cash. I do. Well, I don't really. But I get it after I've seen the Bus. It's a 1963 one-ton, Type 21 F (fire truck), for sale by a factory fire brigade—first and only owners. It has 9,345 km on it. It has the original tires on it, and they have the original air in them. Original paint, you ask? Not only on the outside: the brake drums still have the original paint on them, too; the fire brigade never got them heated up. On the shelf under the ash-tray that's never seen butts is the dealer's warranty check-up booklet for tune-ups and lube jobs and stuff, with half the coupons unused. The Bus slept every night in the heated fire engine bay. After 30 years of faithful service, it is being retired. They want 3,000 D-Marks for it. It is worth five times that.

How often does a grown man regain his long lost childhood— the Idyllic Childhood he wants to remember, childhood as it ought to have been—in time-warp condition, with a full tank? Not often. When opportunities like that arise, there is only one question a man with more than half his wits about him (or at least the ability to summon said wits on 24 hours' notice) would ask: "Do you have any more?" Alas, they did not, so I settled for just the one. Marco and I drive My Childhood to his workshop to prepare it for the German TÜV.

For the benefit of those who may not know what the TÜV is, I shall explain. Every vehicle registered in Krautland is required to undergo a certain ceremony every two years, called the TÜV (rhymes with roof). It is looked upon by Germans with as much relish as a visit to the dentist or the tax auditor. It consists of a rigorous inspection of roadworthiness. Technically, they can flunk you if the license plate bulb fails to light. If anything of a graver nature, such as questionable brake lines, should be discovered, you might as well call a tow truck right now. They can seize the vehicle to prevent it from being a menace to navigation if they deem it less than roadworthy.

Part of the ceremony involves ensuring that the vehicle meets the original technical specifications. Modifications, such as fat tires or bigger carburetors or flared fenders, are not tolerated. That's the theoretical part of it. The practical part involves driving the vehicle over a pit. Down in the pit is a gorilla with an assortment of screwdrivers. His sole purpose in life consists in attempting to pound the pointy end through any body part or frame member which looks like it might yield, and he pursues this purpose with the single-minded thoroughness we both admire and fear in the Teutonic race. This last part of the ceremony is the one which causes most cars to fail eventually, for rust never sleeps.

In anticipation of this, Marco and I check all the light bulbs. Underneath it's clean. He is confident My Childhood will pass muster. But you never know. Thirty years is a long time for a car; rubber and gaskets and hoses and things deteriorate, even when it sleeps in a heated garage.

On the appointed day, when I and My Childhood arrive at the TÜV, we are pleased to note that the inspector is having a light day and appears to be in a good mood. He is pleased to see such a fine old car in such apparently fine condition.

"Turn on the headlights, please."

I do. He can barely see them—6 volt—and makes a note on his clipboard. "Turn on the windshield wipers, please." I do. They swish painfully slowly—6 volt. He makes another note on his clipboard.

"Turn signals."

Another black mark on the clipboard. I might mention that it still meets 1963 specs, so, technically, it ought to pass—but I bite my tongue. Rule Number One: never volunteer information to the government; speak only when spoken to, and only in monosyllables. They will only misinterpret it anyway, if you volunteer them the truth.

"Horn."

H-O-O-O-O-O-O-O-T!! He startles. The fire brigade wanted you to know they were coming. The inspector is impressed. No black mark this time. We go round to the back to inspect the engine. It's not a chromed concours d'élégance winner, but there are no precious bodily fluids leaking out anywhere and no crud caked on anywhere. Moreover, it idles like a purring kitten, no suspicious ticky-ticky noises or colored smoke. The inspector begins to think he might just be able to overlook a slow wiper motor.

"Drive over the pit, please." The gorilla grimaces expectantly, brandishing a halogen lamp with which to peer into every crevice where a speck of rust might hide. He picks out a prize screwdriver. I drive over the pit, switch off the motor, and wait.

Remember *The Fall of the House of Usher?* Vincent Price buries his sister alive in the family crypt, but his supernatural hearing picks up her pounding and scratching inside the coffin and he goes insane. So there I am over the pit, having surrendered the soft underbelly of My Childhood to an insane Vincent Price.

In my mind I hear the pounding and scratching, but the inspector with the clipboard does not. Normally, he expects to. He looks round from behind his clipboard and peers slantways down into the pit at the gorilla, awaiting his verdict.

"LIEBER GOTT!!" the gorilla cries—for the love of God! He has not struck a single blow. My Childhood is pronounced roadworthy. The inspector and the gorilla congratulate me. "I wish I'd had such a nice Childhood!"

The registration papers declare the top speed to be 105 kph. Remember, this is the one-ton version, with low gear ratios. It hauls cargo, but not ass. I strongly suspect that the only time this bus got up to 105 was on the freight train from the factory in Hannover to the fire brigade in Mannheim. On my way home from the TÜV, at night, with 6 volt lighting (more like dimming), cruising at nowhere near the imaginary top speed, I nearly lost My Childhood, again. A careless, perhaps drowsy, driver came up from behind on the Autobahn—where there is no speed limit—and severely misjudged our speed differential. He registered my dimly lit rear end too late to brake. He did the only thing left to do: swerve. He passed me in the other lane still swerving—spiraling like a whirligig, all four tires squealing and smoking. I thought we were done for, but he saved it.

The next day Marco and I decide to convert My Childhood to 12 volts. I also realized that if you try to hold onto something fluid, like time, it runs through your fingers like water. So I added a bit of wisdom to the tailgate window. I am reminded whenever I look in the rear-view mirror, and others are reminded when they come up behind me: all things must pass.

all things must pass
MA
PS 42 H
BUS
BUS

I Almost Bought a Conversion Van

Michelle D'Amico

WHEN I FIRST BEGAN MY YEARLONG SEARCH FOR THE PERFECT BUS, I had no idea it would take me over three years to find the perfect mechanic. True, I do have various factors against me. First and foremost, I am a woman, and second, the only thing I really know how to do is change the oil. Last, the guys I date know only as much as I do.

The trials and tribulations I have experienced with my Bus have never made me want to rid myself of the four-wheeled beast until this summer. You see, when I first purchased my '66 Westfalia camper from a teacher in Eugene, Oregon, he had just had the engine rebuilt. I drove it away with only 200 miles on it. I have gone on to replace nearly everything but the transmission.

The last thing I expected was that I would have to have the engine rebuilt again, only 34,000 miles later! This May I was stalled on the freeway in a typical Oregon rainstorm. I had just disconnected my cell phone service, and I was stranded there with my dog and no leash, and had to carry her several miles to a pay phone. When the tow man arrived, I decided to have the Bus towed to a new shop just three blocks from my house so that I could quickly get home. I left the Bus there for a week waiting for an estimate of the problem. Four days later, the mechanic scribbled me several engine rebuild estimates on a napkin.

In the interim, I had met a "perfect stranger" in a parking lot of a reggae show: a guy who drove the same year Westy as mine. He had offered to help me by donating some engine parts to my notably worthy cause. When I was handed that napkin, the mechanic had already dismantled my engine, which was scattered in pieces all across his shop floor. The "perfect stranger" had accompanied me and advised me to take the Bus to someone else, especially since this mechanic had lied to me about one of his references. (He told me that he had previously worked for one shop for eight years, but in reality, he only lasted one week before they fired him.) I immediately told this guy very nicely that I had changed my mind. (He was trying to steer me in the direction of a $5,000 performance engine.) The "perfect stranger" began loading engine parts into both his Bus as well as my engineless Bus, and we called a tow truck again to have it towed to my usual mechanic.

The mechanic started cussing me out, saying, "Get the @#*! off my property and never come back!!" Okay, okay, I tried to be nice about it but *geez*. We quickly pushed my inoperable Bus out of his vicinity. I then had it towed to the place I had been established with for the past year, the only place so far that could get the job done right the first time around. They had my Bus for two weeks and after the "perfect stranger" donated $800 in parts, my final bill was only $1200 and my new 1600 engine was quite enjoyable compared to the old one, which struggled up the slightest incline at only 35 mph.

Everything was running smoothly until one warm day I was in a record shop and over the loudspeaker I heard, "Would whoever owns the green and white Bus please come to the front counter." I knew that I was not illegally parked so I approached the counter with great curiosity. "A customer says your Bus is leaking a large amount of gas." When I got outside to investigate, I found a very large puddle. I drove the Bus home immediately to give it a rest. I called my mechanic's shop (the one who had just rebuilt my engine), and was told this was "normal." A week and a half later, I scheduled my 300-mile (post engine rebuild) checkup and instructed them to check my fuel tank and all fuel lines. The next day, they phoned me to say the only problem was the gas cap gasket, which they replaced.

A week later, the problem continued, with passing pedestrians still expressing their concern. I phoned my mechanic two more times and I was continually told not to worry, this was completely normal. I always tell my "mechanic of the moment" never to rush, just do the job right. But it seemed weird that he didn't want to address the problem.

Two days before the Fourth of July weekend, it was a cool 55-degree day and gas was literally pouring out like a faucet. Later that night, I had the Bus towed back to my mechanic's shop. I had every weekend in July booked with out of town camping trips and it was just two days until I was due to depart for a Fourth of July holiday weekend at the beach. I was fuming mad and I expressed this in the letter that I left in the shop's mailbox, with my Bus blocking their front door. (It's amazing what a resourceful tow truck driver will do for a lady close to tears!)

I wrote that I expected to be made top priority; I expected to have the Bus repaired and functional by tomorrow afternoon. I demanded that the owner call me at once, etc. The next afternoon, I received a phone call from the shop owner asking, "What do you expect me to do? We won't be able to fix the problem in two days; it would take at least three weeks and I'd have to charge you $800."

At this point, I realized that during my July Fourth weekend, I would have to sleep in my Uncle's minivan at the beach, since the hotel my family had booked didn't allow dogs and every hotel in town had been booked for three months prior. I also had to quickly reserve a rental car. I was NOT a happy camper! I told the shop owner that I felt he had "deplorable customer service skills" and that I couldn't believe he had been in business 30 years and was treating me this way. He just replied, "It's all we can do." I immediately left work and called our local VW club President Burt Reif. After listening to me vent my frustration, he directed me to Ashley at Always VW.

Since I was near hysterics, Ashley agreed to take a look at the Bus, but cautioned me not to drive it from shop to shop but to have it towed again. When I phoned AAA again, they said the tow company refused to tow my Bus with a fuel leak, even though they hadn't objected the night before. I hitched a ride from a neighbor, got my Bus and proceeded to drive very slowly to Ashley's shop, paranoid about what various people had told me could be a dangerous situation.

Once I arrived safely at Ashley's, he said he could fix the problem for $300 and it would take a week. During my Bus-less week, I began contemplating buying a Dodge or Ford conversion van. I even went so far as to get insurance quotes and payment options. There was one big perk: you could use a conversion van as a tax write-off, if you were a homeowner (they qualify as a second home). But just the sight of those ghastly $35,000 vans evoked images of Dirk Diggler lounging on orange shag carpeting while clumsily smoking a roach-clipped joint with feathers dangling from it.

Still, all I could think of were two things. First, I would be embarrassed by this costly eyesore. Second, my Bus is everything I want in a car. From its ingenious design, great looks, plus the fact I can sleep in it, it suits my needs perfectly in every way. All I really needed was a good mechanic! Why should I have to part with the Bus I love on account of disreputable and dishonest mechanics?

In the end, I pursued my goal of complaining to the Better Business Bureau (which I had never done before) about my problem with the shop that failed to fix my leaking fuel tank. We went so far as "mediation" between the owner and a BBB representative. Needless to say, we didn't get anywhere and I knew it was pointless when the owner said it was my fault for not explaining the problem to his mechanic in enough detail! The owner was such a moron that I just threw my arms up and said, "Forget it." However, I posted a sign in my back window for all VW owners to see which warned of these crooks.

Legal? Maybe not, but people who have saved their Splitties, and who might be on a budget, deserve to know. So I will keep my Bus and my sincere hope that Ashley will continue to treat me right and give my Bus the love and care that she rightly deserves.

Our Anniversary

Marek Zebrowski

CAN YOU EVER IMAGINE GETTING A GIFT FROM YOUR BUS? No, really—I mean it—a gift from what many less sensitive souls would see as an inanimate object? Hmmm... interesting... peculiar, you might say, or mumble something to that effect. And yet, I assure you, it happened.

As with all stories, this one has a humble beginning. Imagine a small suburban house and a gray cement garage, freestanding in the back-yard. Rotted remains of the wooden garage reveal the 1965 blue-and-white Bus I came to see. Yes, it was for sale. No, it wasn't running. "Electrical problems," said the owner with a sigh betraying years of frustration. But I, I was ecstatic.

My first visit to the States took place during the summer of 1968 and included, among many other attractions, one I would never forget: a week-long trip from Massachusetts to Maine that included lots of miles in a blue-and-white VW Bus. Ever since then, my childhood dream was to one day own just such a Bus. It seemed to me like the friendliest, most versatile automobile ever made—just the kind that would make a young car enthusiast lose his cool when arguing the pros and cons of vehicle design with his friends. And on that early spring day some 12 years ago, there I was looking at practically the same kind of Bus!

My mind was already made up, but we went through the motions anyway.

"So, it isn't running?"

"Yeah," said Jeff, a student owner, with a trace of disgust.

"What about the interior?" (It was in very good original condition, although the middle bench was missing.)

"Oh, I've got that seat somewhere in the basement."

"Fine. And what about the engine?"

"Second."

"Transmission?"

"Still the original one."

"Right. What are you asking?" (The body was in perfect condition—a California Bus with Livermore dealership plates.)

"$450."

I drew a deep breath and paced around the Bus trying to look
thoughtful. "Will you accept $300?"

"Take it," was the brisk answer in which I sensed relief. And
now the Bus was mine!

I have to admit that the electrical problems have plagued me
for a long time. Yes, I got the Bus running, eventually replaced
the engine with a used one first, and then, more recently with a
good rebuilt one. I also have a new transmission and scores of
other parts that were needed to keep the Bus going.

My Bus transported me—grudgingly sometimes—up and down
the East Coast in all seasons and with all kinds of cargo. I
cannot think of more pleasant beach picnics than the ones in
which my Bus and I have participated. There is no more conve-
nient vehicle for trips to the NY airports to see my cousins off
to Europe, laden with huge boxes and trunks filled to capacity.
And how I relish the winter driving on the turnpike, wind whistling past and trying to blow me across the lanes as I huddle,
wrapped in blankets, tightly clutching the steering wheel and
peering through the darkness beyond the pale yellowish light
cast by the 6 volt headlamps. Not to mention the countless
moving jobs for myself, my relatives and my friends. All these
experiences made me feel closer to my Bus, respecting its needs
and accepting its whims.

With the passage of years, the advanced age of my Bus has man-
ifested itself in several rather subtle ways. First, my Bus developed a fondness for the hair dryer. After the first chill of the
season, his old bones require a few minutes of hot air and gentle persuasion to fire up nicely after turning the key. Then, as
the miles rapidly kept piling up, my Bus simply refused to start

if it didn't feel like going. Rather than bow to the inevitable pressure to reduce my driving, I devised all kinds of schemes to make it go. My neighbors were amazed sometimes to see me push the Bus down my driveway (which is, unfortunately, level), and then, in mid-flight, jump in the cab and drive away. My trips required a grand strategy then—I could only go to garages with ramps or park on streets at such an angle that a push start was possible.

Sensing my determination, the Bus would continue trying to circumvent my driving it anywhere. It snapped the clutch cable twice in one year recently, for example. And it snapped a throttle cable one midnight on Route 128 (here I opened up the carburetor and left it stuck open at something like 2000 rpm and, switching between second and third gears, finally reached the safety of my garage after some delay). Then it refused to allow me to use the turn signals when the headlights were on. (Ah, but I remembered the hand signals required for the driver's license test). And so on.

Please don't think for a moment that ours was an adversarial relationship. Oh no! Rather, it was like a capricious child, this Bus of mine, that required constant proofs of my devotion.

—New transmission??

—*Fine.*

—Tires??

—*Sure.*

—Generator, headlights, bumper, front windscreen (as it leaked)??

—*All replaced!*

—A diagnostic check-up? Cosmetics to improve your appearance?

—*Here you go!!*

Finally, my Bus was pleased. And just in time, too, as I had started to wonder aloud whether I should keep it!

And here is the great proof that, indeed, this inanimate object did express gratitude for all the attention I gave it and suffering it brought me over the years.

One day some months ago I drove down from Boston to Newport, R.I., for the day. It was a sunny, pleasant morning, just the kind of weather Buses like to have for a good exercise. Rolling along Route 24 southbound at a steady 55 mph I was contemplating how fortunate I was to have just such a vehicle for the trip, when I suddenly felt compelled to look very closely at my speedometer. It still held a solid 55. But all the digits on the odometer had vanished! The last one was just turning into a big fat zero! And then, as I stared, it was nothing but zeros, five of them, in fact, all the way to the left! Two hundred thousand miles!! I felt my pulse quicken and my throat was dry.

It is never far from the slow lane to the breakdown lane, so I pulled over and stopped to think about this important milestone, this amazing anniversary.

"*Anniversary,*" I thought to myself, suddenly remembering the date… it was my thirty-fifth birthday. As sweat beaded on my forehead, I could barely formulate the thought… my dear old Bus… *remembered.*

Hundreds of cars kept streaming by, oblivious to this important moment in our lives…

How peculiar, you might say, or mumble something to that effect. And yet, it happened.

All That Plus Evidence of Other Struggles

John Lago

YOU CAN TELL A LOT ABOUT A BUSSER by the way he wears his clothes, but you can tell even more by the way he wears his clothes *out*.

Say you meet a Bus-driving man and he's got big holes worn through the seat of his pants. If he's got patches on those holes and more holes worn through the patches, now there's a guy who's got his Splitty tuned to the point where his main thing is sitting in the driver's seat driving, or camped and sitting on a log while contemplating his next mile.

Then you see a Busser with his knees out. The first thing you think is: here's a guy with a lot of engine hassle. Most of his quality time has devolved into quantity time and is spent kneeling under the engine lid trying to banish that rough idle or tending to the mysteries of flat spots in the acceleration. Maybe he's even doing some praying back there when the mystery gets too deep, or doing some genuflecting, when, as if by divine intervention, the problem sometimes solves itself.

Then, too, you assume a guy with holes in the back of his shirt to be a Busser who likes to do the supine scootch under his ride to wrestle with the tie rods and drag link. If there's a rectangular configuration of oil drips on the front of that same shirt, that garment is likely gracing the back of a Busser who backslides under his Bus in an attempt to stop the leaks around his pushrod tubes with frequent applications of Ace Home Caulking.

Just when you think you've seen all the classic sartorial Bus-inspired tears and smudges, someone comes along whose clothing suffers all that plus evidence of other struggles that defy a standard explanation. It happened to me on a warm day in October when Carl Neuman pulled up in front of my place in a 13-window white '66. "How do you like it?" he said, even before getting out.

I'd heard about his latest deal, but upon seeing it in the tin (which corresponds to "in the flesh"), my first reaction was to glance back in the driveway at my old Bus, compare the condition of it to his, and say, "How 'bout I get you drunk and we switch titles?"

Instead we switched the oil in his tranny. He was on his way to Iowa to get married, and from there he and his bride Jenny were heading out to their new home in Montana by way of Guatemala and Bumph Uque, Egypt, and for that they would need fresh juice in the little underhanging box of gears.

Of course, Carl, of German extraction, baptized in drain oil, and even rumored to have metric nuts, had been a Bus Man since the beginning of the Cenozoic, and man, did it show on his clothes. He had all the aforementioned cuts and imprints, plus an intriguing scattering of tears in the sleeves of his T-shirt and more slashes and holes at the ankles of his jeans.

Before I could inquire as to the origin of those mysterious punctures and perforations on the sleeves and the ankles, Carl had a 17 mm hex in his hand and was already on his back under the Bus doing the Splitty slither in the direction of the tranny plugs.

He never got there. Carl's dog, part Clydesdale, part Chow, and part Two-Connections-Short-of-a-Complete-Circuit, grabbed Carl by the pants leg and yanked him out from under the Bus as easily as Dennis the Menace is pulled away from his vegetables.

But this is where the correlation with vegetables ends.

Instead of continuing to pull Carl, say, to the garden for burial like a normal dog—he let go of Carl's ankle, ran from Carl's posterior end to his anterior end and tried to take a bite out of Carl's face.

All this was very new to me but apparently Carl had been there before. Reflexively he threw up an arm to block the snapping jaws, frustrating the poor devil with a mouthful of cotton T-shirt fiber when what he really wanted was meat.

The puzzle of the perforated pants legs and the slashed sleeves was solved.

What was not solved was an even greater mystery. "Carl," I asked, without really posing it as a question, "Why in the dickens do you keep that canine crocodile?"

"He guards the Bus," said Carl.

So there you have it—Carl Neuman, Bus Man from birth, and with the wardrobe to prove it. On top of all the standard patches, holes, stains, and drips were perforations from an anti-theft system that was as personally dangerous as it was effective. Carl would take a chance with his life, but not with his Bus. He stared death in the eye whenever he looked at that dog, but since the beast kept the Bus from getting ripped off, Carl was willing to put up with the side effects as long as it guaranteed him the right to drive alive.

Driving Tips: VW Buses
And Sub-Zero Weather

Tim Rundquist

WHEN THE TEMPERATURE GETS BELOW MINUS TEN OR SO—sub-Arctic for most places but fair-to-middlin' for winter in Minnesota—the vintage VW engine won't start. It won't even turn over. The cylinders contract from the extreme cold, making the pistons freeze up, making it too mighty a task for the starter to cope with. You're stuck.

One morning in Minneapolis, during an unseasonably cold snap just after Thanksgiving, Dan and I encountered this phenomenon of the frozen engine. We talked over potential solutions (aim a blow-dryer at the engine block? Put the 1967 Bus, and ourselves, in a crate and ship everything to Florida?) before finally calling a Volkswagen repair shop. The mechanic on the other end of the phone, after laughing a bit, had the solution: barbecue the engine. What you do is get some charcoal, light it up in a hibachi or metal garbage can lid, wait until there are no more open flames, and stick the whole thing under the oil pan. In about twenty to thirty minutes, pull them out and start your VW. The heat should have freed up the pistons sufficiently to turn the engine over.

Dan and I found some gourmet briquettes, with real flecks of mesquite, in my uncle's garage, lit them in a garbage can lid and placed them under the VW Bus's engine block. A half hour later, we came back outside, removed the charcoal, turned the ignition, and the engine fired right up. Another miracle of modern technology.

There is only one drawback: the older Volkswagens are "heated" by air ducts coming from the engine. After using the barbecue method, you get into the driver's seat to start your car, and you could swear that Dad is in the back somewhere, flipping burgers.

The essence of Texas mesquite lingered in the van as we headed up U.S. 10 towards Otter Tail County. We thought of red-hot chili and buffalo steak as we drove through snow flurries for four and a half hours, wrapped in our Mexican blankets.

Out of town, into the blurred gray-and-white countryside, up the unsanded country road. Trudging up the hill in the VW van, as if we were on old wooden cross-country skis: moving forward slowly, but steadily, with just enough lack of traction to make things interesting. I have learned, over the course of 10,000 miles or so, to simply trust the VW to get us places, rather than fretting about the conditions: snow, rain, heavy winds, whatever. Things like accidents and breakdowns were not to be expected: there was no set "law of averages" that required a disaster, every x amount of miles. When mishaps occurred, it was simply a fact of life, something to be dealt with, tough bananas: nothing to do with predestination or anything.

Actually, the pre-1968 Buses, and even old Bugs, do surprisingly well in snow. The engine is mounted in the rear, right over the drive axle. What they lack in guts, they make up for in relative traction. Even without snow tires, you can still get most places; put a set of studs on a Bus, and you can go just about anywhere. Provided, of course, you barbecue that engine first.

We reached the top of Hill #1 and drove/skied to the bottom. Across the bridge, over the frozen creek, and there was a mailbox, on the right hand side. A narrow road curved up another hill, through a stand of sugar maples. A single set of tire tracks cut through a foot or more a fresh snow. The tracks were quickly filling up.

There was some hesitation on my part. Was this the place? Could the VW Van, in spite of my confidence, actually make it up this road, given the current conditions? Did this road even go anywhere? Were we going to end up stuck in some frozen cow pasture? Exactly what the hell was so important about finding Dent, Minnesota, maple syrup, anyway?

"Don't be stupid," said Dan. "*Do* it."

So we did. We got up a head of steam, pushing the speedometer all the way up to 15, and charged into the driveway. The VW Van shimmied, lurched, stopped momentarily, then settled into the tire tracks. We slowly chugged up the hill.

Excerpt from 50,000 Watts of Jazz From Fargo, 2001.

Tired of Life?

Rainer Müller

RECENTLY, WHEN I WANTED TO TRANSPORT SOME KIDS in my '57 Kombi, one couple said that their kids could not come along. The Bus was not safe because it had no seatbelts.

A short time later a gas station attendant was telling me of his past experiences as a VW mechanic. After the initial joy at seeing a reminder of his youth, he became thoughtful. Among his many stories of happy customers were also a few horrible memories of crushed legs, shattered heads and other injuries resulting from the early Buses' complete lack of safety equipment.

Feeling decidedly more insecure, I drove my Bus home and parked it in the garage. The following day, after climbing into my new Passat, I paused and studied the interior equipment: automatically adjusting seatbelts, headrests both front and rear, airbags, ABS, collapsible steering column, a large "crush zone" in front, a dash made of skull-friendly plastic, safety glass, and enormously safe handling characteristics.

And then there was my Bus: no belts, zero crush zone, the original 6.40 x 15 bias ply tires, the pendulum rear axle with handling reminiscent of the pitching of a boat, the ever-present steering wheel slop, single-circuit drum brakes, and lots of nice hard steel to knock one's head against. On top of all this, a Bus with a 36 HP engine is a continual traffic hindrance, inspiring drivers of modern vehicles to often-dangerous passing maneuvers.

I sat petrified in my Passat as these thoughts whizzed through my head: "You're responsible to three kids and a wife. You insist that they travel in the Bus. How can you justify the danger presented to your family by your old car craziness?"

The following days were no better. My fascination for old Buses and the accompanying dreams of road trips were constantly undermined by concerns of safety. I was in such a quandary, but then I started to think about some of the intrinsic disadvantages of our modern oh-so-secure times. We find ourselves surrounded by a buffer of assurances, safety precautions and predictable paths our lives can follow, so that danger as such is suppressed and sealed out of our lives. Everything is under control.

I suddenly realized that I don't want this secure mindset, that parts of it were even repulsive. It's as if we are enveloped in a giant airbag! So much is so soft and so safe that no matter how a person falls or how stupid he acts he isn't hurt. The fact still remains, though, that life is life-threatening, and can end in a moment. The more one realizes this, the freer and less encumbered his life will be.

I believe many modern safety measures are an attempt to digitize, and thus allay, our fear of the unknown. An adventure has an element of danger. If there is no danger, there is no adventure!

Advertisers' prattle touting amusement park adventures and experiences is just stupid. Children garner false experiences and are encouraged to participate in over-organized, commercialized events whose results are totally predictable. The most wonderful experiences I have ever had (and continue to have) are those that were dangerous, where something unpredictable could have happened. My story of my reluctant trip down a mountain road on a folding bike with no brakes continues to make a good tale. But no one cares in the least about my account of an amusement park ride.

Everyone needs a true dash of danger. Otherwise one bounces around in this modern, flabby, padded world so long that he has to get his kicks bungee-jumping or vicariously through watching sporting events.

After these strong arguments with myself, I can now gladly climb into my Bus just as it is, without seatbelts.

And I again look forward without reservation to our long planned trip to Greece next year: the whole family, large roof rack, tent and lots of camping gear packed into a Bus with a 36 hp motor as it climbs steep mountain passes, takes hairpin curves and transports us for thousands of kilometers. Yes, I even think my kids will have an adventure to talk about for a long time to come… that is, if they survive!

Translated by Burt Reif

Bus Love

Wimpy, Wimpy, Wimpy!

Lois Grace

WIMPY, WIMPY, WIMPY! Ever heard these words? Of course you have, me too. But then I heard them directed towards my beloved '59 Single Cab, Vernon. It was then that they took on an entirely new, decidedly personal meaning. Can you imagine the NERVE of this guy, to insult Vern while he's standing there within earshot?? I put my fists back in my pockets and sidled closer to ask him what he meant. With Vern weighing in at about 2300 pounds and only 36 horsepower, I should have known what this guy was implying but it still didn't sink in. So when the guy went on, I paid closer attention. He was a nicely-dressed older guy, obviously enjoying the Father's Day car show. He leaned closer to me, and with a conspiratorial smile, he whispered, "WOW. This sure is handsome! Very nice… bet it was a lot of work… but really, come on, REALLY, isn't it awfully, you know, GUTLESS???" I was astounded. I mean, call him handsome, call him ungainly, call him slow, call him ODD, even. But don't call Vern gutless. No. My fists were out again, but I kept my cool. Because, actually, Vern IS gutless. SHHHHHH. Don't tell Vern I said that. What did this guy think I was going to do? Stand there, in full view of my Big Blue Buddy, and announce to the world, that yes, indeedy, folks, this thing couldn't get out of its own way?? I don't THINK so. And, for Pete's sake, he was right there, listening! Listening! He doesn't know he isn't a big, manly kinda guy! He thinks he's a 4-wheeler.

He thinks this way because of the life he's led. After all, up until about 5 years ago, he was a Workin' Truck. So, it's only natural we'd be puzzled when someone refers to him as wimpy. While I have no hidden urges to wrestle an old Type 2 (much less Vernon) around in some mud bog, the things Vern's done in his past make that pale by comparison:

He's hauled endless tons of newspapers to the recycler, along with years and years and years of aluminum and other trash. He's pulled stumps and hauled dirt when we dug a well and gotten stuck in ditches in the pouring rain (getting out under his own power, I might add). He's gone to the dump, for our family and friends and friends' families, dumping ton upon endless ton of garbage—we'd put the sides and tailgate down and shovel the load off, finishing in half the time it took the domestic truck owners to unload their (unhinged) trucks. He's been handy and willing and dependable and capable, and yes, slow. He's been a warm place in the cold, a dry place in the wet, a cool breeze in the heat, and a shining beacon of (6 volt) light in the dark. (Can you hear the violins scraping yet??) He's run hither and yon, for miles and miles and miles, sometimes with very serious mechanical difficulties. But at NO time was he ever wimpy. Underpowered, yes. But never wimpy. Wimpy is sitting in the driveway, with a thousand bucks worth of mud and snow tires, and never seeing anything dirtier than the city street after a good rain. Wimpy is power steering and air-conditioning and back-up camera! Wimpy is big, overblown and underused, all of which Vernon certainly is not. My point in all of this? Well, if it isn't painfully obvious by now, my point is that slow doesn't necessarily equal cheap or useless. I think that is what bothers me most, the assumption that if a truck doesn't have whomptillion horsepower, huge tires, bumpers like telephone poles, and a light bar filled with bulbs (all covered with happy faces, of course), then it can't possibly be a TRUCK. I'd make a small wager that Vern's worked more in his life than these so-called trucks ever will. I suppose, though, by comparison, Vernon and his kind do look a bit fragile. Tiny little engine, sitting back there ticking away, while the gaping maw of the V8 hungrily, demandingly, roars for attention and more fuel. The Type 2's spindly front beam, steering box sitting out there in the breeze, wheels tall and skinny hanging from the ends of the trailing arms, instead of the mountain of rubber and explosion of shock absorbers of the 4-wheel drive. I'd venture a guess that one of these beasts has more square feet of rubber than I have square feet of house. And the face. The placid, gentle, peaceful expression on a flat, bland face, instead of the jutting snout, breathing heat and gas fumes and noise, missing grille or paint or both. I suppose one could draw the conclusion that a VW Type 2 is sort of the automotive Wally Cox, the weenie, if you will. And that guy calling him gutless just stirred all my primitive, self-defensive instincts into play. For, to attack Vern is to attack me.

The guy was still talking while all this ran through my head. He was laughing and giggling about how he, many times, had had to "follow one of these things" up a hill and was wondering if they'd EVER reach the top… and BOY! How slow can you go anyway? Why, my own sister still calls them Rolling Roadblocks! When he paused for breath, I managed to ask him how fast he wanted to get someplace anyway?? I asked him whether the point wasn't just getting there at ALL? He looked at me blankly as if that thought had never entered his mind. You see, he didn't MEAN to be derogatory or demeaning (he really seemed like a nice enough guy), he just had never thought of VW's that way before. As cars and trucks!

Too bad that speed is the gauge by which toughness is measured. If that warped view is true, then the old VW must surely lose. But for those of us who know otherwise, we rest assured that the most important thing about a car is that it will hold together and do what you ask it to do. Vernon has more than fulfilled his duties in this regard—sometimes he was so eager that he actually broke parts when trying to please us. Silly humans.

And, never mind how fast you get somewhere! If speed were truly the issue, you'd be in an airplane and not in an old VW. Volkswagens prove again and again to be a credit to their fine heritage. Never mind manly or wimpy, macho or geek. By my calculations, all VW's are macho. But what do I know? I'm a GIRL.

The Novel Solution

Chris Pollard

ONE OF THE ABIDING JOYS OF DRIVING A BUS, which hasn't been produced for over 50 years, is trying to get ahold of one of those indescribable parts which breaks at the least opportune moment. That moment, in this case, occurred during a hot summer in France, and the part in question… well, that would be jumping ahead.

And so the scene is set. I was lying on my back under the faithful old Bus getting my feet suntanned. If there had been room, I would have scratched my head. The events which led up to this odd posture, a gearbox (or transmission, if you prefer) filled with a perfectly matched set of neutrals, had been progressive and predictable. The deduction of the problem was, therefore, perfectly logical. And completely wrong.

I had had minor problems with the gear selection for a while. The shifting—let's face it, it could never compete with a Swiss-watch when it comes to precision—seemed vague and rubbery even by the undemanding VW standards. I put this down to wear in the joint at the base of the gearshift and resolved to fix it at a future date (read: never), and promptly forgot about it.

The Bus elected to raise the profile of the gearbox problem in decisive fashion. The shift, instead of following the traditional "H" pattern, suddenly adopted a racy and unconventional configuration whereby the two sides of the "H" moved smartly together. Push forward for first or third, pull back for second or fourth. Different, and a bit-nerve-racking, too, as there was no way of telling which gear was going to engage. Third to second was no problem really, as the worst that could happen was to get fourth, which only slowed things down a bit, but fourth to third was exciting, as I had the same odds of getting first, which slowed things down—outside of the engine, at least—a lot. Time to fix this, I thought, before the valves team up with the pistons and make a bid for freedom. So, next campsite, dive underneath for a look around.

Now, on the end of the gear-change shaft just before it vanishes into the gearbox is a little rubber and metal coupling, designed, presumably, to take the shock out of some of the more enthusiastic gear-changes. The rubber had torn through and partly separated from the metal; the shaft could now push and pull without any problem, but it couldn't transmit any significant twist—hence, the closing up of the "H." Ten minutes with the wrench and 50 cents in the swear box (no point in being over generous) and the offending article was off. The small but interested semicircle of spectators applauded gently and wandered away.

I've owned this Bus for a long time, and I know better than to go away less than fully equipped. As well as the usual tools, epoxy and duct tape are an indispensable way of effecting some creative short-term solutions—you know, the kind of temporary repairs which generally outlive the vehicle. Glue the two sides together, bind up with tape, reinstall, and resolve to take it easy on the gearshift. It didn't occur to me to wonder *why* it had broken, or why it had been difficult to get back on. All I cared about was that it had worked. Not exactly Formula 1, but at least the "I" had gone back to being an "H." After all, it was a holiday, and there are more attractive things in Normandy than the oily underside of a Bus. The food and the wine, the sunshine, the beaches and castles—it was back to the life of the sybarite. With glass of wine in one hand and novel in the other, I settled down to watch the sunset. The wine was better than the novel, and I was glad when the sun sank so low as to make reading impossible. Do people make a living from writing such drivel? French numberplates have a better plot. Still, I reasoned the book wasn't very thick, so it shouldn't last long. Thank goodness.

The repair lasted two days of smug self-satisfaction. Normandy roads aren't anything to write home about. Some aren't even anything to go home on and after one particularly deep pothole, the repair let go. Oh well, back to the campsite and through the rigmarole again. Time to try to buy a new coupling. I scoured Normandy for a VW dealer, and in my best French asked him, "Do you have a gear-change coupling for a 1967 VW Type 2?" I now know the French for "No Longer Available," which is what was displayed in large, friendly letters on his computer screen. Back to the sticky tape.

Things went from bad to worse on, predictably, the journey back through Normandy to the St. Malo ferry. This time, the gear-change became progressively more obstructive, and eventually, five miles south of the terminal, gave up completely. Only neutral was on offer. Helpful passing French drivers hooted cheerfully, calling what I took to be words of encouragement. So, once again, onto the dusty hard shoulder, out and under. Off came the coupling and out came the tape.

This time it was clear that the problem had grown up. Having fixed the coupling (again!), there was no way it would go back on. Peering into the oily murk—some VW Bus parts aren't designed to be worked on, I concluded—revealed that the input shaft to the gearbox was a good inch below the shaft to the gearstick. How could this be? How could the gearbox drop down without the front gearbox mounting breaking?

The blinding flash which had been launched several days earlier finally arrived. Of course! The front gearbox mounting *had* broken, the rubber pad sheared away from the metal plate, but so cleanly that I had missed it when looking for the original fault. The poor little coupling had, towards the end, been taking both the weight of the gearbox and the flexing of the transaxle. No wonder it had broken.

This left me with a new and rather more serious problem, namely, how to support the gearbox and reconnect the coupling. It only had to last the five miles to the ferry; once back in England, the recovery service could take me home. But for the moment, that five miles looked like five hundred.

Sliding the trolley jack, another indispensable item of equipment, under the gearbox nose and jacking it up the requisite inch at least put things back in place, but I could hardly drive like that. (I know trolley jacks have wheels, but there are limits.) I thought about building a rope sling to support the 'box, but rejected this as I could find no suitable anchor points. Ideally, I needed some sort of support to take over from the failed gearbox mount.

One of the features of the earlier Buses, which I believe was deleted when they redesigned the rear suspension for the bay-windows, is a U-shaped crossmember which runs under the gearbox just forward of the differential. With the 'box at its correct altitude, there is a gap of around three-quarters of an inch between the underside of the gearbox and the top of this crossmember. Aha! All I needed, then, was a wedge or pad of the requisite thickness, and it would support the gearbox long enough to get me home. But what to use?

I rummaged for some time. Folded up towels, bits of nearby fence post, scraps of metal. Then the penny dropped. The novel! Its only redeeming feature, apart from the fact that we had finished it, was its thickness. Three-quarters of an inch. To fit, it needed sawing in half with the bread knife (anyone want the lower half of a very bad novel?) to slide into place. I thought the weight of the 'box would hold it in, but then thought about torque reversals. Fortunately, there are holes drilled along the crossmember, I know not why, and a self-tapping screw stolen from the front door trim soon had the book anchored securely. Back on with the coupling, and away we went, no worries. In fact, it worked so well that I didn't replace it for several months after that.

An interesting problem; I suppose you could call it a novel solution.

I Was Hauling In My Bus One Day

Clara Williams

THE OTHER DAY, THE WASHING MACHINE BROKE. It had been making a funny noise for a while. Funny-peculiar, not Funny-haha. Sort of a complaining moan. Finally it gave up the ghost and stopped during the spin cycle. A minute later it would click and spin a little, then go back on strike. Somehow, I was persuaded into investigating further (meaning the clothes and excess water had to be removed and the machine vivisected, revealing… a bad bearing. Washing machines, while having in common with VWs electrical motors and windings and bearings, are not really all that similar to VWs, and tinkering with them gives me no joy.

I unplug the machine and turn off the water. Meanwhile the laundry pile grows. Now it piles up to the ceiling…

I open the local paper and investigate the appliances section. I get in touch with a fellow via the Daily Zero claiming to have a perfectly functioning washing machine for sale for a reasonable price. Not only that, he also has a refrigerator. This sounds interesting to me as I have this old fridge. It's one of those that has the freezer inside the fridge. One door. And the freezer section turns into an ice cube. So I have to chisel through the ice to unearth frozen goods. If you defrost the freezer, it really messes up the temps and the fridge gets too cold, and the milk, etc. freezes. I moved it here from the last place I lived, and moved it there from the squat. Yessireebob, this was a squat fridge, from that house in the woods that everyone got evicted from when the foreign absentee landlords showed up one day on a surprise visit, the Sunday afternoon when there had been a three day party going on and there were people camped out in the back yard and various detritus everywhere.

Ten years later I still have this fridge. It is not so modern. It is practically antique. Certainly it's a classic, it must be at least 25 years old. I bet it has collector value. I'll put it on eBay… I'll be rich! Or, I'll put it in the garage and put beer in it.

We get in the red vee doubleyou Microbus and head off to hunt appliances. Made a deal and purchased both the fridge and the washer. The guy asks if we'll come back for them. Well, no. Then he suggests two trips. Huh? I start thinking the small children are a front and he is a fence for stolen goods, and he is trying something shady.

No problem, I say. We'll take them in the Bus. It's rated to haul one-ton.

For some reason your Average Joe is really surprised by this. I don't get it.

Why do they make vehicles shaped like pickups that are wimpy? I was surprised when I found out how few one-tons are out there. Buses are made for hauling stuff and haul they do and can. Some people like old Buses 'cause they want a hobby. Some people have shiny Buses they rarely drive and drive shiny cars or something not an air-cooled VW as a daily driver. Some people drive things shaped like pickup trucks that are rated half-ton. Some people think non-shiny cars don't run. Some people drive old VWs.

Both appliances are put in the Bus and driven home. The washing machine has a piece of concrete in it that makes it really heavy to lift into the Bus. But the Bus doesn't really seem to drive much different. I go easy on the gas so the fridge won't slide into the back window during acceleration. Drove through town, down the hill to downtown, across the temporary bridge (they are tearing down the old bridge, what a mess) up the hill, stopped at the red light, up the hill more, turn right at top of hill and 4 more miles—out of town. Get home and unload the load. Try not to mash the rusted bit of floor by the cargo doors more than can be avoided.

Mission accomplished. Now we can do laundry and keep ice cream.

One December Day

Jim Bryant

MY DAILY DRIVER IS A VANAGON, which I often leave overnight in the parking lot when I carpool to work, riding back with another member of our carpool. But one evening I got a call that my fellow carpooler was ill and wouldn't be making the 40-mile commute the next morning. Plan B was my '67 Deluxe, Potluck. Put away for the season, Potluck doesn't see much winter. It doesn't see all that much road time either. I rebuilt the 1600 hp engine over the summer. I had put maybe a hundred miles on it since then and it had developed an oil leak traced to the main seal. I ordered a new seal and a new flywheel (to match the new counter-weighted crankshaft), figuring I'd pull the engine and make it right in the spring.

I didn't have that luxury this morning. Potluck started right up and I pulled out of the shed on a December morning that wouldn't normally be so balmy. The forecast projected 60 degrees, not exactly normal for Northern Illinois in December. I'd take it.

Sunshine, flat roads and a tail wind. What Bus driver could ask for more? My only bumper sticker reads "0-60 in 15 minutes," but that morning all went well. I had no problem cruising on the two-lanes at 55. I tuned into the sounds of the drive train and enjoyed the ride. Potluck had been on the road since the engine rebuild: three miles into town for groceries or ten miles to the next town. The break-in period had turned up a carburetor problem that necessitated a rebuild of a smaller venue.

A second opinion always increases the confidence factor. My friend Dan had taken it for a country road ride during his stop-over on a trip from Denver to Chicago in a '72 Bay Window Bus. He pronounced Potluck strong and smooth. His friend Tom (the new owner of the Bay) was glad to be a Bus owner on his own, but I think he sensed the extra karma factor of the split-window generation as he rode shotgun during our country motoring excursion, the soft top pulled back to let the sun and wind in.

At 20 miles, the halfway mark disappeared in my rearview mirror. I considered stopping when I passed a disabled Ford pickup with two guys under the hood. I'd left without my toolbox, so I wouldn't be much help. They would be on their own that morning. A few more miles down the road I passed a disabled Dodge Caravan. No one around to see the smug expression on my face as the dead first minivan imposter disappeared in my figurative dust. Ten more miles and I parked nose-to-nose with my Vanagon in the parking lot for the start of the workday.

Convoluted Civil Service organizational theory dictates that the Northern Illinois University staff meteorologist is under Architectural and Engineering Services, of which I'm Director (something to do with safety, I think). Had I been more attuned to that connection, I would have been aware that the conflu-ence of weather conditions, which made my ride to work a pleasant one, would work against me later that day. The west-erlies at my backside in the morning would accelerate as a front came through.

As the work day ended the clues fell into place. My walk to Potluck was a breezy one, but he started right up and we pulled out of the parking lot onto Lincoln Highway, heading west toward home. Though they call Chicago the Windy City, that moniker has more to do with bombastic politics than blus-tery climate. The Hawk, as the locals have dubbed the winter winds, has to traverse DeKalb County and NIU before it ever reaches John Hancock Center, Soldier Field or Lake Michigan. In essence, we're the snow fence for the City with Big Shoulders. Potluck and I met The Hawk head-on as we turned out the parking lot. Even the dropping temperatures were of little con-sequence compared to the head winds: sustained winds at 40 mph, gusts to 60 mph.

No traffic was in sight. There's usually a rush to get out of town at 4:30 and I'd left a bit early to beat it. I shifted through the gears and hit fourth at 35 mph. There I left my foot on the pedal and hoped for the best. The speed limit is 45 mph for about a mile until you hit the cornfields and then the limit goes up to 55 mph. In my mirror I could see a line of cars coming up behind me as I crawled by the "55" sign. I had just managed hit 40 mph and was creeping up to 45 mph. The first side road was still four miles away. By the time I got there, nothing was ahead of me but The Hawk. Behind me, though, were two dozen frustrated commuters.

I was beginning to wonder if my engine was really putting out all it could. Just when doubts about my engine rebuilding ability were overtaking my consciousness, I found the side road, made the right turn and left the water-cooled commuters behind. Driving on the plains of Illinois is not unlike sailing on the Great Lakes. All depends on where you're going. A slightly different tack can make a world of difference. The wind I had fought head-on for four miles now filled my left-rear corner like a spinnaker. I eased my foot off the gas at 65 mph and cruised silently at 60 mph to the next stop sign. My doubts gave way to elation.

Those VW Bus owners who drive curvy, hilly roads from Point A to Point B might begrudge those of us who have straight, flat roads. Don't. Point B is rarely 40 miles in one direction. It's usually 20 miles in one direction and 20 miles in another. Cornfields rarely offer the hypotenuse approach unless you're powered by John Deere. Instead, travel is a zigzag affair, punctu-ated by stop signs.

My choice that afternoon was to go four miles west and then four miles north alternating along country roads. The dead Dodge was still there, unmoved since the morning. I was still moving, but I wouldn't be for long if I didn't stop. On the west-ward leg of the trip, I could watch the fuel gauge needle drop, closing on "R," and a stop was in order.

In the land of F-150s, Blazers and Rams with suspension systems up to my quaint sliding door window, a fuel stop in the social center of Hicksville (apologies to Dan Hicks) means cheap gas and expensive milk at Casey's General Store.

An air-cooled VW Beetle raises an eyebrow. An air-cooled VW Bus means someone has to saunter over and ask, "What year is it?" I've never found it in myself to reply, "Oh, 2010… oh, you mean the Bus." That would be rude.

The first guy to walk over asked the obligatory question and I told him through the sliding window that it was a '67. The second guy left his Harley leaning on the kickstand to point out that I was dripping something from back there. I acknowledged the problem, adding that I knew I needed a new main seal and only had a few more miles to go. He seemed satisfied that he'd spotted a problem and pointed it out. My response appeared to satisfy him, too. Both ends of the automotive spectrum find common ground in the life-blood of motor oil in an air-cooled engine. I turned the key and headed home, leaving a small spot of life-blood next to the gas pump.

Several cold fronts later, I still haven't ventured to the shed to pull the engine and replace the seal. The Hawk will circle my shed for the next few months. Cold steel and numb fingers used to be the prerequisites of staying on the road. These days, I'll take the luxury of a daily driver with a wasserboxer.

The Shape of Busing to Come

The New Microbus

Dan Proudfoot

CELEBRATING THE 30TH ANNIVERSARY of beginning New Microbus production, Volkswagen announced on April 1, 2053 that demand for the retro vehicle with the enduring appeal is showing no sign of easing.

Indeed, production grew to 130,000 in the 2053 model year.

The New Microbus, along with its related truck and Westfalia models, has proved to be a natural compliment to our line of all-wheel-drive sedans, sports cars and luxocarriages, all powered by VW's patented hydrogen boxer motors.

Of course, the 2053 New Microbus is a far cry from the first such vehicles with VW's trademark giant VW insignia on the otherwise little-changed, split-window front.

Older readers will remember the original, 2023 New Microbus was almost as basic as its inspiration, the Volkswagen Microbus of 1967, which had been considered the last of the split-windows until VW brought new life to the design.

Although Volkswagen made its first-generation New Microbus six inches wider and a foot longer than the '67 Volkswagen Bus, in appearance and character the New Microbus was remarkably similar to the German original that research recently has revealed to have been designed by Erwin Komenda, sculptor of the original Volkswagen Beetle and Porsche 356 more than a century ago.

As promised, VW stuck to its pledge of delivering a production vehicle that remained true to the spirit of the prototype that had won the company plaudits at Frankfurt, Detroit and Tokyo auto shows.

Today's basic New Microbus, at $349,000, still utilizes torsion bar suspension and seven-passenger leatherette seating. In many ways it recalls its Volkswagen antecedent, although the switch to hydrogen fuel in 2032 rendered it non-polluting. All New Microbus purchases now include membership in the Sierra Club.

The New Microbus Deluxe at $549,000 now accounts for the vast majority of sales. It's widely known as the 42-Window, referring to the multiple oblong windows above the vintage-effect rain gutter, a feature now emulated by competing van manufacturers. Clear glass, polarized or open-air options are deployed by driver control. Less obvious are the solar panels integrated into the remainder of the roof.

Among other features developed by VW, ground clearance varies automatically according to speed. Alternatively, the "Load" setting compensates for carrying cargo up to 3,000 pounds.

Sliding windows in the front doors retain the character and practicality of the original Volkswagen, yet many owners admit to preferring the six-unit climate generators that deliver cooled or warmed fresh air to each seating position.

The seats are lighter than those of competitors and can be removed effortlessly: their frames are made from carbon fiber, even though seating surfaces retain the spring/horsehair construction of half a century ago. Options include buckets or bench in the front, two- or three-passenger seating in the mid-row, and a three-person rear seat that folds into a bed.

Vintage VW Bus enthusiasts are quick to point out that Volkswagen's success over the past 30 years has all to do with the New Microbus retaining the vital characteristics of the old Volkswagen. "We should all thank our lucky stars the decision-makers in Wolfsburg gave up on their idea of a front-engine Microbus just after the turn of the century," said Mike Robus, VW Bus historian. "They had the decency to confer with vintage Bus aficionados before proceeding in its development, and every one of our ideas was adopted."

"Pivotally, the development of hydrogen as a fuel helped assure the Bus's appeal," Robus noted. "If the combination of hydrogen fuel cells and electric motors had proved to be the panacea expected in the dying days of petroleum power," the historian explained, "the internal combustion engine would have gone the way of the dodo and the tuna fish. But breakthroughs in hydrogen compacting and storage facilitated the simpler solution of using the non-polluting substance to power engines once fueled by gasoline."

"A New Microbus has a characteristic sound that's music to our ears," Robus continued. "Of course, the music of an original Volkswagen's air-cooled mill is the equivalent of chamber music played with the original instruments, but the water-cooled, hydrogen motor is the modern equivalent, and still quite unique. You hear and rejoice in the thrumming of a New Microbus coming and going. The quiet humming of an electric motor would never have cut it."

As stated earlier, the New Microbus is six inches wider than the VW Bus on which it's modeled. Improved stability in crosswinds and more predictable handling were the goal as engineers set out to make the New Microbus capable of the 100 mph speed limits instituted in 2040.

The increase in overall length, originally controversial among Volkswagen enthusiasts concerned with any change to their beloved chariot, has become accepted as necessary in order to meet (and exceed) modern crash safety standards. The extra foot is entirely in the nose, and accounts for some of the most innovative engineering in the vehicle. In the event of an impact, energy is absorbed by other-universe materials and transferred beneath the vehicle. Yet the "face" of the vehicle appears exactly the same as that of its vintage Bus ancestor.

"For too many years I've thought of my knees as the crush zone in my 1964 Microbus," admitted Dan Proudfoot, who at the age of 111 still likes to take his like-new '64 on the country roads surrounding Toronto, Ontario, Canada, on sunny days. "Nowadays I buy helium balloons and pack them in front of my shins, taking the place of old-fashioned airbags, but when I was younger, I just didn't worry about the risk. I was having too good a time."

Proudfoot gives full credit to Volkswagen for its achievement, yet stubbornly refuses to join the legion of New Microbus enthusiasts.

"Good as they are, I prefer the original," Proudfoot concluded. "Besides, a New Microbus may be worth every penny of its

$349,000 price tag, but as any vintage Bus enthusiast knows, a rust-free original like mine is worth $1,000,000. And it's still appreciating!"

Note: This story was updated from the original by the editor.

Very Wild BUS

Stewart Alcorn

Article originally published in Metal Kar magazine, May 2057:

THIS MONTH'S FEATURE METAL KAR is a really wet 1963 Volkswagen Bus. Originally produced 100 years ago, these were the "groovy" cars to have if you were a hippie back in the late 1960's. The early history of this Bus has been lost in haze of the marijuana smoke of its time. Jim Socks, the current owner, found the Bus in a neighbor's yard being used as a dog kennel. "The interior was trashed, it had these weird opening windshields and the exterior had these really ugly EMPI five-spoke wheels on drop spindles and an iridescent paint job. Obviously, it had been customized back around the turn of the century and it looked really ugly." Well, Jim has certainly taken care of this Bus.

The doggie-smell is long gone and now the interior provides calm, quiet composure. Driver and passengers relax in La-Z-Boy seats equipped with "Sense-A-Round" stereo components, seat heater/coolers and Magic-Fingers. The driver's seat also includes the "Wide-Eyez" anti-sleep stimulus package for long road trips. Installed below the dashboard is a three-line beverage dispenser and throughout the Bus are cup heater/cooler holders for the 2-liter "Bladder Buster" mugs. The beverage reservoir is located in the engine compartment where the original gasoline tank was, and the reservoir filler cap is behind the old gas flap. Now tanking up for a big ride means no one goes thirsty.

The driver and front passenger look out windows of "Transitions" glass, so no need for sunglasses as today's high UV levels are completely blocked. To retain that vintage look in the forward cabin, Jim retained the old steering column. Even the stereo looks retro, with an exposed original iPod Mega and a NOS Kragen CD player which are connected to a hidden Blaupunkt "Terra Tuner" stereo system. Jim, who got a box of old Compact Discs from his Uncle Moss, says "There is some great artwork on the covers and they sound really funny when they skip." Those skips can sound pretty loud through the Bose "Oil-Coil" speakers and a "Richter Scale" sub-woofer mounted in the belly pan. All together the stereo produces an amazing 212 decibels when Jim wants to really power his favorite band, the Free Radicals.

All the windows in the rear passenger area have been replaced with video screens. Each is independently controlled so Jim and Lucy's spawn can either watch the outside world go by, play v-games, or watch movies. Jim says that Bobby, their youngest son, "loves to play the same Disney movie on each screen, each one about 30 seconds behind the last. That way he can see his favorite parts over and over." To utilize their kid's abundant energy, Jim installed the "Sibling Rivalry" Play Power generator. "When the kids are really feisty, we'll strap their hands and feet in and have them play 'Slug-Bug' to power up the video equipment." The video screens display the normal traffic outside and splice in those old VW Beetles from the turn of the century. "Setting the traffic to have about 10 Beetles a minute really juices it up."

Since Jim is a federal Peace Maintenance Officer, he has all the required safety items in his Bus. At each door are the "cancer causer" warning stickers ("Materials found in this vehicle are known to cause cancer in CA, NY, MA and OR") and similar "brain basher" stickers ("Enter vehicle at your own risk: vehicle interior constructed of materials which could cause injury or death in the event of a collision") warning stickers required for all Metal Kars. Also, the driver's door displays a sticker that states "Experimental vehicle: Driver must possess a license for the operation of class 17 vehicles." Since this is no parade car and Jim wanted to maintain the 250 kph pace mandated on today's freeways, he installed the "Envelope" collision protection system. Since this Bus was built long before the system became a standard feature in 2025, Jim had to install the onboard processor, all the required video cameras, and interface the system with the steering, acceleration and braking controls. He also installed the "HTG" (Home To Grandma's) programmable destination autopilot with voice activation. Talk about riding around in comfort—you don't even have to pay attention to the traffic.

The old combustion engine wasn't going to be able to cruise at today's freeway speeds, and Jim didn't want to mail order for a few liters of gasoline every time he wanted to go for a drive, so he replaced the smog-maker with a Pratt and Whitney S5000 hydrogen turbine engine which powers a Bosch "Flash Power" generator. Electricity powers the Bosch "Electron Torque" motor to turn the JC Whitney "Starburst" wheels wrapped in Goodyear synthetic tires. Most of the power plant is "Kromed" and it all fits within the space of the original engine. Since the silent Bus just didn't sound like a Metal Kar, Jim installed "Faux Pipes" coming out the back which play a recording of an old air-cooled VW as he heads down the road.

Stepping outside you'll notice that "PlastiKrome" bumpers and light bezels from JC Whitney are found at both ends of the Bus. The window cut-outs in the rear passenger area have been filled and smoothed for the wet look. All the doors are servo-controlled so the latches have been removed as well. Jim took full advantage of the large amount of flat real estate on the sides of this Bus. The entire Bus below the belt-line is covered in "Flexi-Pixl" video screens. These 1 mm thick screens are bendable over two dimensions and will adhere to any surface. To pay the credits Jim owes for customizing the Bus, he often runs advertisements on these screens when he is zooming about town. But on weekend drives you'll see faux flames shooting down the side of the Bus as Jim burns down the road. This old hippie Bus might even inspire a flashback to the 1960's, when Metal Kars ruled the road.

Bus Phantasmagoria

Night of the '54 Barndoor

by Ron Van Ness-Otunnu

THE AD APPEARED ON THE INTERNET BULLETIN BOARD AROUND 7PM. The poster, thousands of miles from me but linked in the spirit of the Bus hunt, had found a fresh ad on some obscure corner of the 'Net that simply read "'54 Barndoor Volkswagen van for sale, $750 OBO." The biggest shock of all was that the phone number was in my area code. But there I was again: logging on over an hour after a super deal was posted to the Bus-hungry masses. Feeling that I had already lost out, my heart sank, yet I optimistically began to dial. I should make it clear that I'm really not like those other Bus fanatics. No, I have a measure of self-control—one Bus is good enough for me. But as I always say, there's no harm in looking, and my intentions were unselfish: after all, I'd potentially be "saving" a Bus. Who knows what kind of horrific customized fate lay ahead of the poor old Bus should it not reach my loving arms? I quickly canceled my date for the evening and stationed myself by the phone in the bedroom, dialing and redialing the number listed in the ad, as it remained unanswered. Hours passed and my eyelids grew heavy as I lay slumped over the phone, a pathetic figure whose head rested on a half-eaten bag of Cheetos. By now it was past 2 AM and with little remaining strength or hope I knocked the phone off the receiver and managed to target the redial button. The ringing stopped and after an eternity of silence, a soft voice answered the call. I perked up and babbled something slightly incoherent about a Bus for sale.

"Oh yes, the Bus," a pleasant male voice replied. "It's still for sale." I leapt off the Cheetos, sending cheese dust across the wrinkled bed sheets.

"Can I see it now?" I shot out impetuously. My mouth had awakened before my brain, costing me the cool edge that a savvy buyer should have. When it comes to Buses, my negotiating wits turn to jelly. Before I could recover, I heard the man's good natured laugh and a "Sure, you must love vintage, original VWs," on the other end of the phone. A subsequent exchange of pleasantries revealed that the seller, Bernard, had just completed the seminary and was selling the Bus (which had belonged to his late father) before leaving for missionary work in South America. "My father loved that vehicle and had all sorts of gadgets for it," said Bernard. After a pause he added in a seemingly caustic tone, "He liked to keep everything original." He continued in a pleasant voice. "But it is, after all, just a material object and I estimate its fair worth value as transportation and all the miscellaneous items to be about $750, but I'm willing to negotiate."

My mouth grew dry and my palms began to sweat. I felt deep within that Bernard was sincere about this Bus and for once, I was the lucky first caller on a great bargain! Bernard was still talking as I drifted out of my reverie. He was saying something about how he was looking forward to the challenge of his missionary work.

"Yes, you're right; it's the use value of the Bus that counts." I said automatically. I was a bit off topic at this point in the conversation but Bernard was forgiving.

"You say you'd like to see the Bus tonight? Well, I'm a bit of a night owl these days; I suppose I could meet you out at the farm." We calculated that we could meet where the Bus was by 4 AM. It was a rural area and I knew the route vaguely but had never noticed the farm off the road that Bernard described. The tools were already packed in my '71 bus and I happened to have an appropriate tow bar handy (just in case I ever had to help another Busser in need).

I reasoned the scenario was perfect: Bernard would leave to meet me and would therefore miss any subsequent inquiries by persistent Bus seekers. I was somewhat confident that Bernard wouldn't sell the Bus out from under me, but who knows what manner of wily character might persuade him to break our agreement? Yes, I preferred the advantage I possessed.

The only route that led to the small town where the Bus was sheltered was unlit and narrow. Fortunately, a full moon burned brightly that evening, lighting the path to my prize. I turned into the narrow dirt drive just at 4 AM and my generator light then began to glow. Well, at least I'd made my appointment. Getting back might be a challenge, though, and at this

Illustration used with permission, ©James Ellis, 1997

point I began to realize my intention of making it to work by 8 AM may have been a bit optimistic.

The path grew narrower and steeper as I forced the Bus past the overgrown brush on its edges. As I made the final ascent, the moon shone brighter than ever directly into the large window of my '71 bus, lighting my face. I crested the hill and the farm yard lay before me, my headlights illuminating the scene as best as my failing generator would allow. The buildings were ragged. I slowly navigated around the debris and old farm equipment that littered my path. It was then I noticed the shiny black Cadillac hearse parked before an old barn. A man, darkly clothed, stood alongside the car. He was looking toward the ground, but raised his head slowly into the direct glare of my lights. At first it seemed his face was blank, but as I blinked in disbelief, I began to discern thin features and the hint of smile. I stopped the Bus fifty feet from him and sat there idling for awhile. This was not how I had imagined Bernard, and for the first time that evening amidst the clamor of my expectations I grew cold and felt suddenly vulnerable. As the man walked in my direction I reached for the shifter, but just at that moment the '71's engine stammered and died. I quickly turned the key but the engine refused to turn over. By then the man had reached the side of the Bus and I felt his stare as he peered into my open window.

"Ron, I presume?" It was Bernard's voice. I turned slowly and fixed on his pale face. His features were somewhat grim and he seemed years beyond the twentyish man I had envisioned. He wore a brownish sport jacket over a darker outfit and his body seemed to blend into the night.

"A hearse?' were the first words that came from my ill-prepared lips. I tried not to sound afraid, but the atmosphere was overpowering.

"It's practical transportation for me. I find it very useful," was his response.

"So, the Bus is in there?" I said, pointing at the barn.

"Yes, shall we?" With that Bernard opened my door and I crept out into the desolate landscape.

My mood of enthusiastic anticipation for the old Bus had turned to a dark foreboding. We walked slowly toward the barn when Bernard stopped abruptly, jolting my already heightened senses. "Why don't you take this flashlight and have a look at the van, I'll join you shortly. I left some paperwork in my glove box that you might be interested in seeing."

I took the light and aimed it toward the slightly open door of the barn. The flashlight caught something bright and it reflected back at me. For a moment I forgot Bernard as I realized it was the bright paintwork on the familiar shape of a Barndoor Bus. I approached quickly and entered the structure and shined the light directly on the Bus. Incredible! A quick glance above the split windows to see the ventless roofline confirmed that I was in the presence of a true Barndoor Bus that had somehow been spared the ravages of time. It was a delivery model and had the special order rear hatch without glass. I dropped to my knees and felt the rocker panels as I ran the flashlight along its side. Perfect! As I stooped lower and ducked my head below the chassis, I discovered that the cross members were pristine.

At that point all I remember hearing was the sound of dry hay break behind me and something whistling through the air. Before I could turn, I felt a sharp pain at the back of my head. I dropped the light and all grew dark and silent.

As I lapsed in and out of consciousness, I perceived what sounded like rain on a roof. When I next opened my eyes, it was still dark, but I was no longer on the ground. I felt the coldness of steel against my cheek. I groped in the darkness with one hand and attempted to raise myself with the other. I kicked something with my knee and reaching for it, discovered the flashlight. Clicking it on, I saw I was lying inside the '54.

Despite my confusion I couldn't help but marvel at the perfection of the interior. The paint was immaculate. As I scanned the interior something strange above my head caught my eye, and I pointed the light upwards. The roof was caved inward: strange, for such an otherwise perfect Bus. I raised myself and stumbled toward the cab section. What I thought was a fiberboard partition was actually a steel panel welded to block the cargo area from the front. I studied the paint and welds. It appeared to be a factory job, but I couldn't recall that option. Despite my distress, I found myself wishing that I had my M-codes book with me now so I could verify this oddity. Then reality set in. I was trapped in this '54 Barndoor and Bernard was not the good fellow he had seemed on the phone.

In a panic I rushed at the cargo doors. They seemed to give slightly but felt blocked from the outside. I made a second run at the doors and this time they gave a bit more, but I fell to the floor from the effort and dropped the light. On the cargo floor near the door line, dark soil had sifted into the bus between the now damaged doors. I stared at the soil and began to tremble: for the first time I touched the dented roof and realized I could not push the dent out. There was weight behind it. I fell back against the cargo floor with the realization flooding my brain: Bernard had buried me alive in this Bus.

I was flooded with a sense of my impending death, but forced myself to examine every inch of the interior to judge for weak spots. I mustered my energy (and the remaining oxygen) for the task of kicking near the cargo door hinges. How I wished there were some rust in the panels to make this effort easier. A grim realization began to dawn on me: I would have to destroy the Bus in order to save myself. At first every blow felt like sacrilege, despite the circumstances. After a while, I experience a kind of catharsis: as I continued kicking at the metal, I watched the pristine cargo door transmute from its original perfection to dented, scarred sheet metal. The dirt that fell loose on all sides of the doors was etching into the factory paint. Although the Bus had cheated the elements for over fifty years, it was now rapidly bowing to wear. I braced my body and kicked frantically at the doors for what seemed like hours. I made slow progress as light-headedness set in.

I made one last mighty kick and the door finally gave, but I managed to break my right ankle in the process. I now had access to the packed wall of earth that lay behind the one broken door, but I did not know how deep I was buried or if I had the strength to dig out of my grave. I pulled the one broken door inward and soil broke free and rushed in. I fell back and again felt the excruciating pain in my ankle, which had been caught in the tumult. My face contorted from the pain. I was bathed in sweat and had been working in the dark for the last hour when the flashlight had broken. I was a blind, wounded maggot now,

filling the cargo interior with armfuls of richly fertilized soil, dig-
ging upward and balancing in the chaos on my one good leg.

The interior was soon shoulder high in dirt but the tunnel to
freedom seemed unending. My nostrils were plugged with filth
so I no longer perceived the earth's stench, but with wet breaths
I sucked soil into my palate. Approximately ten feet above the
roofline of the van, with one ankle completely numb and my
body quaking, I finally poked my fist through to the airy surface.
I jostled upward and rolled my body onto a field. The autumn
sun was just sinking below the horizon.

I don't know how long I lay there, but when I was able to sense
more around me, I realized my '71 van was parked nearby. I
dragged myself toward it, opened the unlocked driver side door
and pulled myself inside. I flinched as I looked back to the
cargo area at the familiar steel interior. Even though this Bus
had windows, it now felt too much like a crypt. I turned the
ignition key and the engine came to life. I drove haphazardly
across the field, double clutching as one useless leg lay still. I
found my way back to the main road and managed to reach a
hospital in the next town before collapsing at the wheel by the
emergency entrance.

A police investigation revealed the number in the ad was to a
pay phone. I was questioned numerous times about why I was
out there at 4 AM. They didn't understand how a fifty-one-
year-old van could lure me out to an abandoned farm late at
night. I can no longer explain it either.

They found the '54 as I had described, buried in the field. When
they pulled it from the ground with a crane in the daylight it
looked nothing like it had the night I first saw it. It was covered
with rust and dents. The once-fresh paint was badly oxidized,
almost as if it had been buried for years. A subsequent excava-
tion of the field revealed dozens of vintage cars—Dusenbergs,
Packards, Pierce Arrows—each with human remains inside.
Strangely, most of the bodies were sitting upright at the wheel.
The causes of death was presumed to be asphyxiation, as if the
occupants did not want to damage the vehicles to make their
escape and had settled instead for an eternity at the wheel.

Since that night I considered selling or junking my '71 many
times. I never thought I'd camp in it again. Some time passed

and I realized that Volkswagen was in my blood and I had to
find a way around the fear that baleful evening had brought
upon me. I decided to modify the '71 considerably: I installed
remote-controlled exploding pins on all the door hinges and
even cut a few emergency escape hatches in the floor and bodywork, not to mention adding hidden compartments for weap-
ons and tools. I can now sleep in the van, but the nightmares
persist. My vintage friends think I'm crazy: the Bus was perfectly original before my modifications. But I've seen enough
originality to last a lifetime.

SPLAT!

Stewart Alcorn

IF YOU ARE A VINTAGE VOLKSWAGEN ENTHUSIAST, or a car enthusiast of any kind, you should have been there. It occurred a couple years ago at the Vintage VW Meet in Seattle. The Professor and I checked out the usual line-up of nicely restored Beetles, Ghias without dented noses, and immaculate camper Buses. But soon we wandered over to where the crowd had gathered, around a new entrant, a 1962 Deluxe Sunroof Microbus. That Bus was so pretty that it easily took first in Buses and best of show. The guy who got second in Buses, who had dumped a ton of money and produced a beautiful Westfalia, was last seen pouring gas all over his new rig before screaming "You have failed me!" and tossing a match on the front seat. The '62 Deluxe was the embodiment of every car collector's most vivid wet dream.

The Bus looked as if it had just rolled out of Hannover, and in a sense it had, for this Bus was unrestored and it still had the new VW smell. Iron oxide and this Bus had never shaken hands. The engine purred and had never let a drop of oil fall from its shiny magnesium alloy case. The bullet turn signal lenses were not crazed, there was no fogging or bubbles in any of its 23 windows, and each piece of vent trim was straight and unscratched. The floor mats were not scuffed, and the rear seat frames were not scratched where they are bolted to floor. The steering wheel wasn't cracked and the horn button was perfect. The owners manual had never been opened. The service record book had never been stamped because the Bus hadn't been on the road enough, the speedometer read 537 original miles! Naturally we were all dying to know the story behind this cream-puff.

The owner, Bob Luckystiff, explained that the Bus was purchased back in the late spring of 1962 by a couple in their fifties. They had seen these Deluxe Microbuses around town, fallen in love with them, and decided to buy one as a picnic cruiser. The Bus was stored indoors during the winter but during the summer they would drive it to nearby parks for picnics with family and friends. Considering how long the summers are here in Seattle you can understand how the Bus racked up so few miles. Sadly, the husband died about four years after they purchased the Bus: he contracted acute food poisoning after eating unrefrigerated potato salad during one picnic. The grief-stricken wife parked the Bus in its storage area and never drove it again. She passed away recently and since their children are materialistic corporate yogurt-brains, who drive SUVs and Teslas, they were not interested in the Bus and an ad was placed in the paper. Bob saw the ad and on the day before the Vintage Meet he bought the Bus—for $500. He hadn't even had time to wash it before the show, but so what.

Well, the crowd of VW junkies was enthusiastic, but they were silenced when the Professor exclaimed "Oh my God, it's a *Automeris floramasticatus.*" I was the only one to respond, saying "What? That can't be." You see, at the time I was a graduate student in entomology (the study of insects) and the Professor was guiding my studies. What the Professor had found, splattered on the front apron of this magnificent Bus, was the remains of a moth that had appeared to have gone extinct in the mid 1960s. Living versions of the caterpillars were voracious feeders and were the scourge of 18th century farmers. Although *Automeris floramasticatus* was an important insect pest in its day there were only a few preserved examples left for science. Back in the late

1950s the noted Dr. Whifflepoof had gathered all but three of the worlds *Automeris floramasticatus* specimens for a sexual dimorphism study when his assistant went mad one night from inhaling fixatives and blew the laboratory up with dynamite. By that time *Automeris floramasticatus* was very difficult to find and only one other specimen was ever gathered for science. The buff-colored *Automeris floramasticatus* was similar to the more common Io moth (*Automeris io*) but with lovely dark blue bands on the wings. Like the Io moth it had a large "eye spot" on the hind wing to startle potential predators. The Professor asked Bob Luckystiff if he could have it and Bob, who didn't really care about the remains of some bug on his Bus, agreed. The professor carefully scraped the remains off the Bus and placed them in a small vial (entomologists always carry small vials in case of finds such as this). For the next several weeks the Professor was in a state of absolute bliss and numerous colleagues dropped by his lab to view the priceless remains. Although it was natural for the Bus to end up in every VW magazine, it also made the cover of Entomology Letters (Vol. 176, No. 3, 1998) along with a photo of the *Automeris* remains.

As the weeks and months passed the Professor's demeanor turned from bliss to scientific interest to downright paranoia. He became convinced that his coveted *Automeris* remains would be stolen by a Canadian entomologist, Dr. Philip LeMaggot, who had countered several of the Professor's theories in the past. The Professor eventually decided that the only way to protect his find was to have more than one specimen. Since finding the remains of other *Automeris floramasticatus* was pretty much out of the question (not that he didn't make me go out and search people's attics and the front grill of dozens of old junkers) he decided on the Jurassic Park approach. Never mind that farmers throughout the American continent were thrilled when *Automeris floramasticatus* was declared extinct in 1971 and would panic if it was reborn like a Phoenix rising from its splattered carcass on the front of a Microbus, this was science. He contacted a geneticist at our University who was studying the genetic similarities between modern elephants and extinct woolly mammoths. They worked out a strategy to remove the nuclear material from the fertilized eggs of Io moths and replace it with DNA extracted from the *Automeris floramasticatus* remains. If all had gone well the insects that hatched from those eggs would have been the first *Automeris floramasticatus* to see the world in about 30 years. Unfortunately those 30 years were not easy on the *Automeris floramasticatus* DNA.

At first everything appeared normal and the Professor was back to his cheerful self. The caterpillars that grew from those hatchlings voraciously consumed the spinach and rhubarb leaves they were provided and their plump blue and white striped bodies looked like the photographs of *Automeris floramasticatus* caterpillars. The few that the Professor would allow us to dissect had an internal anatomy similar to that of Io moth caterpillars. Everything was going well when the caterpillars finally spun their cocoons for the long over-winter wait for the spring. During the winter I finally defended my thesis on the auditory nerves of the deer fly (Chrysops vittatus), proving that their ability to hear humans at a camp site is directly correlated to the development of their blood-sucking mouth-parts, so I was gone when the moths emerged. But I heard about it.

The moths emerged after the Professor had gone home for the evening. When he checked on them the next morning, as he did every morning, he was mortified. His current graduate student said the Professor went berserk and hurled the flask containing the moths at the wall. The glass shattered and the moths began to fly about the laboratory. Unfortunately, the recreated *Automeris floramasticatus* was not a strong flier and is easily buffeted by gusts of wind. It is therefore not surprising that the moths were sucked up by the air handler in the lab and blown out into the crisp morning air.

The older farmers in the surrounding area were very concerned about this release of a genetically engineered nemesis. Since I had recently graduated from the Professor's laboratory and had intimate knowledge of this moth, I was hired by the US Department of Agriculture to study this organism and find a way to again eliminate it. At first, we all hoped that the poor fliers would have been all eaten by birds or bats and not had a chance to mate, but fate is never that kind. Last spring a farmer brought in three moths and I collected two around street lights. Although the reincarnated moth bears a resemblance to the original *Automeris floramasticatus* it is now considered a new species, *Automeris samba*. The genes controlling the development of the head of the moth were apparently the most effected by the

30 years the *Automeris floramasticatus* remains were pancaked on the front of the Bus for it is this portion of *Automeris samba* that has been altered the most from the original version of the insect (see illustration). This change is no doubt what upset the Professor so much. The marking on the wings have changed as well. Several geneticists that I have presented the *Automeris samba* specimens to have not been surprised by the mutations. A component of the Glassurit paint used by Volkswagen from 1960 to 1963 can intercalate DNA strands, allowing mutations to be produced when the DNA was again replicated. This last spring I captured an interesting mutant of *Automeris samba*. It was a stronger flier, capable of increased speed and greater control, and instead of the two square eyes on the front of the head it has a single broad eye.

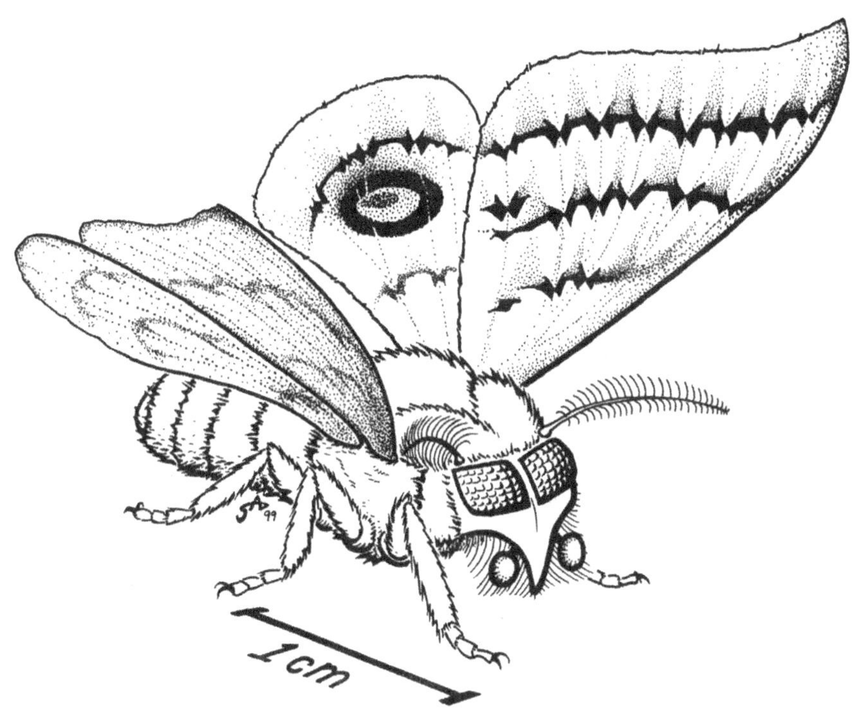

The 5th Van

Ken Wilford

IN A SMALL AREA LIKE CUMBERLAND COUNTY, SOUTH NEW JERSEY you get to know people. If you are a vintage VW fan you get to know the few people that own old Volkswagens in our area, at least by sight. But if you are a rabid VW van addict like myself you get to know the three other people with vans in your area on a first name basis. And so it was, before a chilly night this past December, I was pretty confident in the fact that I was one of an elite group of three other VW van owners all of which belonged to our little club, Jersey Owners of Transporters (JOT for short).

But that night was when I first saw the Fifth Van, and after that nothing was ever quite the same.

I was going to night classes at our local county Vo-Tec to become an Aircraft Maintenance Technician. My experience with VW's came in very handy since most small airplanes still use air-cooled engines. Anyway, I was late for school and had to rush out the door and consequently was going rather fast when I saw a set of strangely familiar-looking headlights coming toward me in the distance. I pulled up at the stop light where Rt. 49 meets Gouldtown-Woodruff Road. There is a small cemetery there and it always made me a little uncomfortable at night having to stop and wait for what seemed like eternity for the light to change. But as I waited, those headlights got closer and finally stopped right across the intersection from me. My VW radar had been correct. It was a VW van, but not just any van. It was a split window and in very good condition from what little I could see in the street light. Split window vans and South Jersey's high humidity just don't get along, so they were very rare to say the least. In fact none of the members of our club owned one and we all were looking to find one to restore with no luck.

I wondered why I had never seen this van before. Maybe he was only a visiting relative come early for the holidays or here on business.

As the light turned green and we started across the intersection simultaneously, I flashed my lights at him, the traditional friendly gesture of fellow VW owners. Not only did I get no response but the van roared across the intersection at a surprisingly quick rate (I was just over the line when he passed me). Looking in my rearview mirror, I could only see tiny dots for brake lights.

'Wow! That thing must be from the '50's!' I thought.

Two of the other three members of JOT happen to go to school with me. Doug owns a '74 Bus and Jerry owns a '79 Bus. So of course when I got to school one of the first things I did was spread the news. It didn't have the result I thought it would.

My friends and fellow Volks folks didn't believe me.

"Are you sure that you really saw a splittie?" Asked Doug with a puzzled expression on his face. "I came down that same road just a minute behind you and I didn't see anything."

They both didn't believe me and I couldn't prove it. As we worked on our projects that night, I wondered if I had really seen it—maybe it was because I wanted one so badly, I just confused another van for a VW in the dusk light. I didn't think about the fifth van again until I saw it again a couple of weeks later.

I was usually early for school and, again, this night, I was late. I had stopped at the same stop light and was fiddling with the radio trying to get the station I wanted. When I looked up, there it was, its large white, VW symbol standing out against the pale blue of the body. I couldn't make out who was driving although I squinted and stared. I could only see an outline through the windshield of what appeared to be a man. I decided to flash my lights before the light turned this time, that way he couldn't ignore me and pretend it was because he didn't see me. Again, no response. I also noticed that the tag on the van was a type I had never seen before. It looked to be antique, which some avid restorers bought and put on their vans to make them more authentic looking. As the light turned green and we passed each other, I really made an effort to see the person behind the wheel. But could only get that shadowy outline of a medium-sized man.

I didn't tell the guys at school about what I saw this time. I needed proof or they would undoubtedly scoff at me again. I believed that the owner of the van must be returning from work and would pass by that spot the same or close to the same time every day. I would have to set up a time for me, Jerry, and Doug to be there watching when the van would pass by.

The chance came when I discovered that next week our teacher would be out of town for a day and we would have the night off. I scheduled our monthly JOT meeting for that night.

And so it was, on that Thursday night, Jerry, Doug, Royce (the other member of the club) and myself sat in my Vanagon next to the cemetery on Gouldtown-Woodruff Road.

"Do we have to park right here?" Doug asked, looking a little nervous.

"This is the spot where I see it and so I know it will come by here." I affirmed. "What are you afraid of? 'Ghost Van' is going to get you?"

Nobody said much after that. Time went on and soon it was a half an hour later than when the van had previously came by.

"I am getting tired of sitting here," Royce said irritably. "Obviously this mystery van is not going to show and I have to work tomorrow."

I agreed that it didn't seem that the van was coming and that we should call it a night.

The next night at school, all I heard from Doug was how I made him sit in the cold next to a cemetery because I couldn't admit that there was no such van. Jerry wasn't so harsh, but he too still doubted my story and was unhappy about the "wild van hunt."

I had to have proof about the van. A way to prove it existed. The next time I saw it, I would follow it.

A month went by. I had almost forgotten about the fifth van. We were working on a tough, labor intensive project in class that kept us all very busy with little time to talk. I had left the house without my books and had to turn around, after getting half way to school, to go home and get them.

I was very late that night and the intense project filled my thoughts. I almost didn't notice the van passing me at the intersection, I was that engrossed. Suddenly, I slammed on the brakes. Fortunately, no one was behind me. I did a quick U-turn and the chase was on. That van was really moving! In fact, I almost thought I had lost him when I saw those little red dots far off in the distance. I stepped on the gas and tried to narrow the space between myself and the van. I held myself at 65 mph. I didn't want to get a major ticket, yet I had to see where the van went and it was doing at least 70.

It had to stop at a four-way stop near the Millville Airport, so I could see that it was going straight towards the Laurel Lake area. I tried to get as quickly as I could through the four-way, and then continued the pursuit.

I saw the tail lights become obstructed as the van went around the bend to go over the Laurel Lake bridge. Then it sailed on past the lake toward Mauricetown. It was heading towards the bay. I followed those two little red eyes to Mauricetown, and that is when something strange happened. I was far behind him and really could just make it out, but it seemed that the van went past the Mauricetown bridge and continued on up to the street that led to the old bridge. There was only one problem. The old bridge didn't exist anymore. It had been a drawbridge and had been replaced in the '70s by the taller, modern bridge only a mile upstream. I thought at first that he must live there on that dead end street. But when I got there and looked around the van was nowhere to be seen.

Suddenly, a strange idea occurred to me. What if it was a ghost van after all? If it was, then it would be on the other side of the river by now, so following this hunch I went back to the bridge and went over the river toward Dennis Township. I was flying now, doing 75 mph and straining to see something.

Ahead there was a Wawa and a Texaco on either side of the road. I seemed to just see the shadow of something van-shaped turning there onto Rt. 47. I turned also and just saw the van turn again into the road that led to Leesburg. Following this road at a high rate of speed, I caught occasional glimpses of my quarry around the twists and turns. Finally, on a straight-away, I seemed to see the van turn into what must be a driveway. I tried to judge where it had turned, but with it being night and the distance the vehicle was in front of me, I just had to guess. I pulled into the yard of a small yellow house with a dilapidated looking one-car garage. I was pretty sure that this was the place, but where was the van?

Someone came to the door.

"Can I help you?" An old man stood there, his hastily thrown-on flannel not fully covering his tee-shirt.

I walked up to the door.

"Yes," I said. "I hope you can. I am looking for a van that seemed to have pulled into your driveway."

"Van?" The old man looked confused. "The only van I know anything about is old 'Betsy' in the garage there and she hasn't seen the road for quite some time."

"What kind of van is it?" I asked fearing I already knew the answer.

"Go look for yourself, but don't touch nothin' until I get a heavier coat on." He turned and shut the door.

I got a flashlight from my glovebox (a must for Vanagon owners) and slowly walked toward the ramshackle garage. Through a crack in the partially opened door, I could just see the reflection of some glass.

"You can't see anything with the door shut!" The old man had come up behind me so quietly that I jumped when he spoke.

I grabbed onto the rusty door handle and he grabbed the door edge and together we slid back the sagging door on squeaky rollers. My flashlight fell on a tremendously dusty and yet familiar-looking VW split window van. You could hardly tell it was blue and white, it was so dirty, yet there it was.

The old man (who was named Bob) explained to me later over some coffee that the van had been his son's before he went to Vietnam. The young lad had asked his parents to keep it for him until he returned. When he didn't, they kept it as a reminder of their son and with a hope that since he was MIA that someday he might return.

"My wife just died this last September," Bob explained. "My kids want me to sell this place and go to a high rise apartment building with other folks my age. I have been thinking a lot about it, but I didn't really know what to do with Jimmy's van."

To make a long story short, I now own the van. It's a '55, and I've restored it completely.

I have tried to figure out exactly what happened that night in these few months that have followed, but I can never come up with a satisfactory answer. Was it the ghost of Bob's son come back to relive better days? Or the van itself drawing me there in hopes that I would free it and allow it to again roam the countryside? Or was there some other explanation?

I thought I had found the answer when I pulled into the Wawa near Leesburg last week for a cup of coffee and did a double take. In the parking lot sat a blue and white '50s-something split window van that had been immaculately restored!

I went inside, and since it was very early in the morning there were only a few other people in the store.

A man stood at the counter and I noticed the keys in his hand.

"Is that your van out there?" I inquired.

"Sure is, why do you ask?" The man looked at me questioningly.

I explained that I had one just like it at home and he went on to tell me that he had recently moved into the area and was now living in Leesburg. In fact he was living on the same street as Bob.

'Aha!,' I thought. 'Now I have figured it out.'

It wasn't anything supernatural. I just picked the wrong house, and by some strange twist it just so happened to be the one where Betsy was residing. A very strange coincidence, but a coincidence nonetheless.

I was getting my coffee and still talking to the guy when I happened to mention seeing his van up in Bridgeton near the cemetery.

He looked at me stupidly and asked, "I know this sounds dumb, but since I just moved here last week, where is Bridgeton?"

The Stories Behind
the Stories

The Origin of the VW Bus

Dan Proudfoot

BEN PON'S VISION OF THE VOLKSWAGEN as a Bread Box as well as a
Beetle changed forever the world of transportation.

Full credit to Ben Pon. But one must look beyond him for perspective in appreciating how the Type 2 came to be a phenomenon far eclipsing any expectations for a boxed Beetle.

The original Dutch distributor for VW following World War II,
Pon also was the man Volkswagen delegated to introduce the
Beetle to the United States. His most significant achievement,
undoubtedly, was sketching the outline of the Type 2 in 1947
and making a case for its production. Three years later was
born the Transporter/Kombi/ Microbus/Station Wagon/
Van-of-a-thousand-names. We're still rejoicing. Type 2's are forever young—and so are we, so long as we keep driving them.

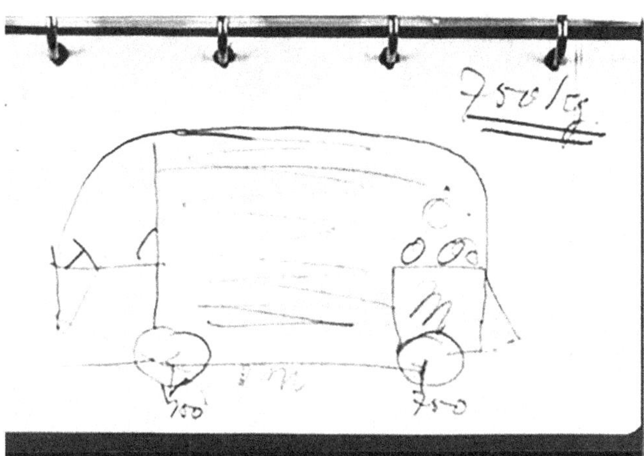

Ben Pon's notebook sketch

The visual appeal of the original, 1950-1967 Type 2—the personality basic to the box, if you will—is at the root of its sig-
nificance in vehicular history. This contention forms the basis
of the piece you're reading, rather than another chronology of
window counts and suspension improvements.

Details of the vehicle's evolution are readily available on the web—from the first prototype delivery vans cobbled together in 1949 through to the final air-cooled van rolling off a Brazilian assembly line in 2005. The birth of the Split Window is all that matters here. Everything else just followed. Begin by recognizing Pon was but one player in the process. Long before his vision was put to paper, Volkswagen's factory workers had fashioned in-house trucks and it was these that most likely inspired Pon during a plant tour. After his sketch sparked VW management's interest, it was up to Porsche, performing research and development on Volkswagen's behalf, to realize Pon's dream and make it production ready.

Study the face of a Type 2. This researcher believes that what comes across is character closely related to that of a Porsche 356. The interplay of curves, the headlamps appearing as eyes, the subliminal suggestion of a sheet metal smile, all are characteristic of the work of Porsche body designer Erwin Komenda.

1951 Bus and 356 Porsche

This cannot be confirmed. But Komenda's granddaughter, Dr. Iris Kinstner, believes it to be true. "My mother told me she often saw her father drawing the characteristic front part of the VW-bus in Wolfsburg," Dr. Kinstner said in correspondence with this writer in 2005.

Erwin Komenda and daughter Ingrid

"In addition, Erwin Komenda often stayed with his family in Wolfsburg—surely not on vacation." In 1949 he traveled to Wolfsburg from Gmund, Austria, where Porsche operated through the postwar years before re-establishing the company in Stuttgart. Komenda spent almost a year there along with other Porsche engineers—none of them holidaying.

The first eight delivery vans that Volkswagen revealed in 1949 were ungainly boxes. The further-developed (almost certainly with Komenda's styling) Type 2 subsequently was aerodynamically optimized at the wind tunnel of the Technical University of Braunschweig. Whether Komenda was in charge of this work is not known, although it seems likely given his previous wind tunnel work with the Type 1 in the same wind tunnel in the 1930's.

Komenda also would have been assigned to Wolfsburg in his role as Porsche's chief body engineer. He'd have been responsible for preparing the Type 2 for mass production and addressing problems as the assembly line began gaining speed.

But any involvement on Komenda's part—or Porsche's—is not confirmed by Volkswagen or Porsche. "Unfortunately there is no evidence on the designers and the engineers of the Type 2 available," Dr. Manfred Grieger of Volkswagen's corporate history department in group communications, replied in a letter when asked directly about Komenda's role following my correspondence with the granddaughter. "Due to the fact that the corporate archives have only been founded in 1997 there are large gaps because there has been no systemical (sic) archiving until that year. Furthermore… not all of the documents have been registered and made accessible yet."

One possible reason for the lack of clarification is Volkswagen's long-time insistence, under managing director Heinrich Nordhoff's leadership, that the Type 2 was the first Volkswagen designed in-house. But as respected historian Karl Ludvigsen notes in his book, *Porsche: Excellence Was Expected*, an agreement was signed on September 17, 1948, with Porsche agreeing again to serve as a design consultant to Volkswagen, taking effect in early 1949.

But long after the fact, it's impossible to establish who did what. Porsche prospered over the years taking on engineering projects for other companies with the condition of confidentiality. As well, the key contributors in Porsche's employ always understood that whatever credit their work should accrue, it'd go to the firm rather than them individually.

Komenda on left, Porsche on right

Moving on to the next step in Type 2 chronology, who deserves credit for the Bay Window of 1968? All that's certain is that with its utilitarian face it lacks the Komenda flair (while retaining some of the details elsewhere from the Split Window). Komenda clearly had nothing to do with this vehicle: he had died of cancer in 1966, all too soon after having retired early, distressed over finding himself in a reduced role as a result of a third-generation Porsche, F.H. (Butzi), establishing a styling department.

The Volkswagen 1500 notchback sedan of 1961 and Squareback wagon of 1962 on the other hand, do look like Komenda designs characterized by smiling faces, clearly defined fenders and faultless proportions. The fastback variant of the car, introduced in 1966, does not. Another Volkswagen best forgotten, the 411, could only have been designed by a committee, never a man as gifted as Komenda.

Some design cars. Others produce mobile sculpture the appeal of which grows with every passing decade.

Taking into account his granddaughter's comments, viewing the evidence at hand, it was Komenda who gave the Type 2 the mirthful personality that so fetchingly compliments its maximal capacity, just as he had designed the Type 1 with a basic shape that at the time wasn't entirely unique but with artful details and forms within the metal that made it something close to a work of art.

It's this writer's impression that every generation of the Type 2 grew more industrial, less whimsical, in design. Not to say that a 1991 Vanagon, for example, isn't a superb vehicle, entirely appealing with its businesslike rectangularity and remarkable functionality, with a strong following of fans who'd drive nothing else. But ask yourself: Will such a Vanagon ever inspire a character anywhere so charming as Fillmore in the movie, CARS? Will the Vanagon ever be identified with a generational movement, as the Split Window was with the hippies? Or inspire copycat vehicles?

No, no, and definitely not. The Pon-imagined, Porsche-realized Type 2 won over so many mainstream Americans through the 1950's that Detroit responded with the 1961 Chevrolet Corvair Greenbrier and Ford Econoline. When Chrysler invented the minivan in 1984, they really only were reinventing the Type 2 Microbus.

But somewhere along the way Volkswagen lost the way. The Routan minivan it put on sale in North America in 2009 (and has compared in Routan advertising, to its shame, to the Split Window) was identical but for badges and interior details to the Dodge Caravan manufactured in the same Chrysler factory in Windsor, Ontario, Canada.

Volkswagen's own vans in Europe, meanwhile, have become as difficult to distinguish from competitors' as Routans are from Caravans. Another Ben Pon, another Erwin Komenda, are desperately needed to step forward with another Type 2, although the new electric ID. Buzz has echoes of the original Type 2.

Additional information:

Josef Kales, Volkswagen's longstanding chief of its development department and a long-time friend of Komenda, certainly would have been involved as the leading engineers of the two companies worked together.

Josef Mickl, chief theoretician at Porsche, almost certainly supported Komenda in shaping the Type 2 because he was an outstanding aerodynamicist.

Dr. Iris Kinstner (*née* Steineck), granddaughter of Erwin Komenda, authored the Komenda Memorial Website: http://www.komenda.at

Author & Artist Biographies

Stewart Alcorn (Very Wild Bus and Splat!)
1964-2015

Back around the summer solstice of 1964, a fresh, new Stewart Alcorn was brought home from the hospital in a 1963 Beetle. His earliest memories often involved trying to see out the back-seat windows of a 1966 Squareback to see what was happening in the San Francisco Bay Area (though sources say this is a lie because he usually was too busy picking on his younger brother. Besides, there was nothing to look at back then in the Bay Area). When Stewart was finally getting big enough to see out the windshield from the back seat his folks traded in the old Squareback for a fresh 1971 model, and those damn high-back seats foiled his new view. The addition of a 1973 Squareback didn't help much, but at least he got to spend more time in the front passenger seat. Sometime in there the family moved to Southern California and Stewart's thoughts turned to fishing. As the elder son, he was bequeathed his Grandfather's car when he became senile… the grandfather, that is… Anyhow, Stewart bombed around in his 1968 Plymouth Fury III for several years until he realized that pumping water through an engine was just wrong, no matter how much power and heat it translates into. By this time Stewart was retaking Beer Drinking 101 at Oregon State University and in a fit of sobriety sold the Fury and bought a 1970 Squareback and an *Idiot's Guide*. Soon afterwards there were car parts scattered everywhere, Stewart was covered in grease, and his parents decided he needed a new car. And not just "a new car," but any car he wanted—after all, he had somehow managed to graduate. To their horror he chose a 1963 Deluxe Microbus (had to have those corner windows). Somewhere about this time he must have bathed since a nice young woman named Susan began hanging out with him… and for some reason she continues to do so. In a masochistic fit Stewart decided he needed to go to graduate school… in Maryland. Obviously, the best way to get a Microbus from Oregon to Maryland is to drive it. So Stewart put 13,000 miles on the bus getting from Point A to Point B during the summer of beer, ditch-weed, fireworks and tequila (did I mention the beer?) Anyhow, after Stewart spent a few years beating his head against the brick walls of the University of Maryland, the Dean decided to take pity on Stewart and make him a "Master of Science." Since Stewart was now over-educated, his first decision was to move back to the West Coast. Again the Microbus took him across the country and he and Susan ended up getting rained on in Seattle where Stewart got a job as a fish biologist, studying the immune functions of salmon for the USGS. He was able to milk that job for about 12 years before the funding went to Iraq. Recently, Stewart has taken a job with the Washington State Department of Fish & Wildlife in Olympia, where he continues to look at sick fish. Since getting back to the Northwest, the Microbus has gotten to rest in the garage, while a total beater 1969 Beetle, another Squareback, and finally a Y2K Bug dealt with the daily commute. In the very late '90s Stewart decided that if he was going to continue to use the Microbus it needed a thorough rejuvenation. And so once again, car parts are scattered everywhere and Stewart is covered in grease.

Everett Barnes (Daily Driver Delusions)

Originally from California, Everett currently resides in Phoenix, Arizona and works as a computer programmer. Since purchasing his first VW as a teenager, Everett has owned more than 25 VWs. His current VW stable includes a 1963 Deluxe Microbus and a low mileage 1963 Squareback in near mint condition. Together with his wife Jennepher, he administers TheSamba. com, a large VW website he created in 1997. Everett's hobbies include collecting VW literature, searching for more space around the house to store VW parts, and watching movies.

Jim Bryant (One December Day)

Jim was raised on VWs, first learning to drive in a 1965 Karmann Ghia. The first wheels of his own numbered two: a 125cc Honda. When he graduated to four wheels, his choice was a '65 Dove Blue Kombi, which lasted until he graduated from college. There he encountered the '67 Velvet Green and Pearl White Deluxe that, two years later, would be his for the paltry sum of $300. The rust was free.

The Deluxe became a ten-year project and the subject of a series of restoration articles. It is still a daily driver, work horse and member of the family. Along the way the Deluxe was joined by other projects: a '67 Double Cab, a '67 Westy, an '84 Vanagon, and a few other examples of the air-cooled persuasion. They all reside, along with his original '68 Honda, on nine acres in the northwest Illinois countryside.

Now retired after 32 years at Northern Illinois University, Jim designed a dream house which he and his wife built in 2007. He already has his dream Bus, his dream girl (Deb, his bride of three years) and a good start on converting an old grain elevator into his dream VW shop. Completion of the new house will set him up for some very golden years rebuilding VWs and, he hopes, learning the secret to running them on a green fuel.

Kristen Caven (Spirit of '76)

Kristin is a writer living in Oakland, California. Her website is www.kristencaven.com. She found a model of "The Road Hog" in a toy store a few years ago but couldn't decide which family member to give it to. Finally, her son discovered it — and now the dream lives on.

Michelle D'Amico (I Almost Bought a Conversion Van)

When Michelle was a young girl, her toy car collection far outnumbered her dolls. Her first toy electric cars were Volkswagen Beetles which ran on a figure 8-style track.

Michelle bought her first real car, a 1973 VW Beetle at age 14 before she had even gotten her permit or driver's license. She has always driven vintage European cars (Mercedes and MGs) until she finally purchased her dream split window, a 1966 VW Westy at age 24.

She reluctantly sold it after owning, slowly restoring, and driving it for 11 years. She then bought and now currently drives a 1985 VW Vanagon Westfalia. She remains quite satisfied with the Vanagon Westy, as it has heat and very comfortable seating. She calls it a "Cadillac" compared to her '66 Westy, though she admits that it's no "looker" and she misses the attention that her '66 used to get.

Jim Ellis (artwork for *Night of the '54 Barndoor*)

A lifelong resident of Phoenix, Arizona, Jim Ellis continues to create Fine Art, Illustrations, professional Photography and share his thoughts, views and twisted insights through his creative writing. Once deeply entrenched in the Volkswagen world, he walks to his post-retirement job and owns a worn out 1993 Ford. Open to a GoFundMe drive at this point, he would prefer a new Toyota 4x4. Ellis, at one time, wrote and drew satirical content under the *nom de plume* "Rusty VanBondo." The character was originally based on an imagined self-deluded "guru" who was responsible for every bad hack and "customization" of otherwise now collectible air-cooled Volkswagens.

Tom Forhan (*Kombi at the Crossroads*)
1947-2019

Tom bought his first Bus in 1968 from Kearny Mesa VW in San Diego for $1495: a 1961 seven-passenger deluxe hardtop in the very popular Beige Grey and Sealing Wax Red. An impoverished student, it was his home for much of the time through college and grad school. As a result, he developed severe Westfalia envy.

He finally did get that camper, a wonderful 1990 Syncro Westie, in 1994. He also owns a 1964 Standard that's been patiently awaiting restoration in a nice dry garage for ten years or so.

Tom works in Washington, D.C. as a congressional staffer. His wife Michele is a translator and their 17 year-old son Colin is learning to drive the Syncro. They live in Takoma Park, Maryland, in a big old house; one of its best features is the two-car carriage house with a huge attic and a driveway that has hosted as many as 21 Buses at a time.

Lois Grace (*Wimpy, Wimpy, Wimpy!*)

I come by my Volkswagen obsession honestly: it's in my DNA. My father was a fan of all things VW, and bought a new 1957 Beetle at the beginning of a lifetime of VWs. In 1967, Dad bought the beat up 1959 Single Cab that would soon become "Vernon." From the moment I saw that truck I was in love with it. I'm not sure why, except it looked more like a new friend than a truck to my 11-year-old eyes. I was hooked, forever. When I drove it for the first time in 1968, I had no idea Vernon would play such a huge part in my life: writing columns for VW newsletters, joining VW clubs, making new friends in the hobby, writing that column for a national VW magazine, and the pinnacle of all air-cooled endeavors… seeing my faithful old friend restored to glory, over a period of 2 years. Since Vernon, I have added 4 more Volkswagens to my family. But Vern remains special. Our ride continues, more than 60 years later. We both have a lot of miles left to travel. Together.

John Lago (*Better, Best, More Better, and Most Bestest* and *All That and Evidence of Other Struggles*)

John is a Splittie driver from way back, although both the Splittie and the driver always needed work. John drives alive in Oshkosh, Wisconsin.

J.P. Henriksen (*My First Drive in a Bus*) 1945-2020

J.P. is an old-school collector and driver of vintage VW Buses in Albuquerque, New Mexico.

Jean-Paul Jacquet (Bus Farming in Rhode Island)

J-P teaches art at the Pomfret School, Pomfret, Connecticut: https://jeanpauljacquet.com/. He also runs a drawing program in France (drawinginfrance.com) for the last 13 years and is renovating an old house there.

Michael Kluckner (Mid-Life Crisis Bus Story)

Michael Kluckner grew up in western Canada and worked for alternative newspapers and as a newspaper cartoonist and commercial artist before commencing a long career writing and illustrating books. His most recent book, The Rooming House, is a graphic novel of hippie life in British Columbia and San Francisco. https://www.michaelkluckner.com/

Rick MacCornack (Truth & Beauty)

Rick has lived on Vashon Island, Washington for 17 years where air-cooled VW transport is still quite common on the many unpopulated rural roads. He has been an air-cooled VW nut for 40 years and currently owns a '63 Karmann Ghia convertible which is slowly making its way back in a ground-up restoration. His biggest regret is selling his very original '67 Deluxe Microbus, which now lives in Tacoma, Washington, where it has been treated to a full restoration.

Raffi Minasian (The Family Bus)

Raffi is a widely published automobile designer, illustrator, writer, historian, Pebble Beach Concours d'Elegance Class Winner, and professor at the California College of the Arts DMBA program. His twenty+ year career includes aircraft interior design for Boeing, toys for Mattel and consumer products for Honeywell, Polaris, and Rainbird. He's designed cars for Toyota, Subaru, Moal Coachbuilders, and The Franklin Mint. His work has been featured on numerous automotive television shows and he has achieved the "Award of Excellence" from *Car Styling* magazine and was part of the design/build team for the

2005 Americas Most Beautiful Roadster "Sedeuced." Raffi has authored articles for numerous automotive magazines and his specialty manufacturing business has made thousands of reproduction parts for rare collector cars for over 20 years.

Rainer Müller (Tired of Life?)

Rainer is a master organ builder and restorer in Merxheim, Germany, and is the proud owner of a 1957 VW Bus. Rainer had long searched for an old VW Bus and discovered his Bus thirteen years ago in a scrap yard in Frankenthal, Germany, rusty and overgrown with moss. It had formerly been in the service of Frankenthal's fire department. For two years, Rainer worked tirelessly on the old Bus: the electrical system was repaired, and the transmission and engine overhauled. The rust was removed and the Bus repainted.

Asked if restoration of an old car was not technically too much for an organ builder, Rainer laughs. "Technology is fun for me, and with an old car you can see how everything works. New cars, with all the electronics, are something else entirely."

Why did he want to own a VW Bus? "The VW Bus was the workhorse of the economic miracle in Germany," he recalled. "In the '50s hardly a company didn't have a VW Bus in its fleet." Rainer, as a craftsman, believes VW Buses and crafts go together. In his youth, Mueller dreamed of touring the world. This also connected it with the VW Bus, because traveling and camping in the sixties was closely associated with the VW Bus.

Chris Pollard (The Novel Solution)

Chris's Bus writes: I was born in 1967, but I don't remember much about my first owner. He pushed me to the back of a barn when his kids got too big for us all to go away together, which is where Chris found me in 1976. He was a penniless student then, studying in London, but he cleaned me up, and we had a lot of fun together. We used to travel out of London at weekends, to the south coast of England, with his girlfriend, and I could tell you some stories about what went on, but I expect he would get cross if I did that. When he got a real job—I think he was kicked out of college, actually, having failed to write up his Ph.D.—I took him to Suffolk, a nice part of Eastern England, where we have lived ever since. Chris has put on a few pounds since then, and lost some hair, and traveled all over the world (he calls it work, but I'm not so sure) but all in all, he seems to have weathered the years okay. I take him gliding sometimes, which is one of his passions, and he took up motor racing a few years back, too—a bit much for us both, with him around 50 and me around 30. I think he works in television now, building satellite systems, but he really wants to be a writer. He sits in the back for hours, scribbling in an old exercise book. One day he'll take the plunge, I'm sure. In the mean time, he's still not married, though I met his new girlfriend recently, and she seems really nice. She said she would make me some new curtains. Maybe she will be the one. Well see. (OMK 797E, on my owner, Chris.)

Howard Pitkow (School Colors)

Howard owns and operates Wagenwerks, a VW (and other makes) repair shop in Wyndmoor, Pennsylvania.

Keith Price (The Treasure Bus)

Brand loyalty was handed down in my family like an heirloom or a recipe. In the early 1960s, my parents' affinity for Volkswagen products coincided with the phenomenal and intelligent Doyle, Dane, Bernbach advertising campaign and the rise of countercultural consumerism. In our flat-roofed house, driving a rear-engine vehicle was as important as poetry and literature, the hi-fi in the living room and Ray-Ban sunglasses.

During World War II military service, my father developed an appreciation for the simplistic elegance of horizontally opposed air-cooled engines in both VW vehicles and shaft-drive BMW motorcycles.

Keith fondly remembers childhood summers spent roaming around with his parents in a 1966 Type 2 VW Campmobile, toting a kayak, hauling antiques, attending VW Club of America picnics, and even traveling to Alaska on the Alcan Highway.

The impact of my folks' VW enthusiasm on me at an impressionable age was significant and profound. They were emblematic of the people that were drawn to the Volkswagen brand in the late fifties and early sixties. My two teenage kids are VW enthusiasts. For three generations of our family, both new and used VWs have been inexpensive, durable, efficient and full of good-humored character. Volkswagens are vehicles you can drive, race, modify, rally, repair, camp in or live in. How many brands can offer all that?

VW ownership can sometimes signal vaguely liberal sensibilities. You will be considered a conservationist and environmentalist—even if your vintage Beetle or Bus leaves a grapefruit-sized oil spot where it's parked. The economical efficiency of VWs can be taken to extremes, like the pizza delivery guy I know in Toledo, Ohio, with 350,000 miles on his 1986 diesel Jetta. He runs a 50-50 mix of diesel and grease that he gets from a Chinese restaurant. Longevity can be counted on and becomes a point of pride. A well-maintained VW of any age can make odometer readings irrelevant. Several cross-country trips in 200,000- and 300,000-mile vehicles have shown me this. No worries, anyway. Availability of VW parts is as diverse as fairground food. The community of VW clubs, events and fellow owner tech help supports the ownership experience in a way that current automotive marketing customer relationship management initiatives could never engender.

VWs were made to run on the autobahn. Engines tend to live long lives because, from an engineering standpoint, they are understressed. A long, healthy, understressed life is a noble objective, and it makes me want to be more like my VWs in that regard.

Within the VW experience, the friendships I've made and the sense of community I have shared have become every bit as significant as my destinations.

A long, strange trip? Bring it on.

Keith Price has been the director of sales and marketing at AutoWeek, public relations manager at Volkswagen of America, currently a product copywriter in the domestic auto industry.

Dan Proudfoot (The New Microbus and
The Origin of the VW Bus)

Born to a father who gloried in ever-larger General Motors cars with automatic transmissions and V-8 engines, Proudfoot's first act of rebellion (and demonstration of pre-teen wisdom) was declaring the Volkswagen the ideal automobile.

Years passed, his affection for Professor Porsche's handiwork never waned. A seven-year-old 1959 Beetle was his first. There followed a 1966 Beetle (purchased new), a 1963 Porsche 356B (truly a super Beetle) in 1968, a 1500 Sedan, a 1957 Beetle rescued from a field, and several more including his favorite year, a 1969.

Too absorbed as a workaholic sports reporter to join the hippie movement in the sixties, Proudfoot came to admire split-window Buses from afar. And then one day in 1993 nirvana finally knocked: a fellow automobile journalist showed Proudfoot the 1964 Bus sitting in his garage awaiting restoration. It was for sale.

With a 12-volt electrical system and a fresh 1.7-litre motor, this Bus became a delight to drive (save when cornering or braking). No other vehicle could match its power in producing smiles among passersby of all ages.

It was sold to a new custodian in 2007 after Proudfoot became enchanted with yet another super Beetle, a 1978 Porsche 911 SC, and found himself needing room in his garage and budget. He misses the Bus madly.

Proudfoot holds the distinction of becoming the first motorsport beat reporter for the Globe and Mail in the early 1970s, where he doubled as the hockey writer. He also wrote for the Hamilton Spectator, Toronto Telegram and UPI. A story in Toronto Life magazine on attending his first racing school earned him an early award. Proudfoot later joined the Toronto Sun as motorsport reporter and columnist but took early retirement following the death of his brother, Jim, a long-time Toronto Star sports editor and columnist. He continues to write on automotive subjects for the Globe and Mail. Dan is hugely respected in the racing community, so much so that when Paul Tracy was inducted into the Canadian Motorsport Hall of Fame, he asked that Dan do the honours.

Flash qFiasco (My Childhood)

After graduating Magnum Cum Nada from the School of Hard Knox, Flash drifted to Europe where he toodles around in the firetruck. Further adventures can be seen and read at http://www.crumplezone.de

Tim Rundquist (Driving Tips: VW Buses and Sub-Zero Weather)
1962-2014

Tim is an attorney and legal editor by trade, and author of two novels, *50,000 Watts of Jazz from Fargo* and *How Heavy is the Mountain.*

Ron Van Ness-Otunnu (Night of the '54 Barndoor)

Dr. Ronald Van Ness Otunnu practices Emergency Medicine in Attleboro, Massachusetts.

Ron's obsession with a 1971 Volkswagen Westfalia began in 1990 with a brief $100 purchase followed by long hours of wrenching and learning. For the next ten years he and his wife toured stretches from Nova Scotia to Louisiana in their slow moving van. In between vacations, the trusty Bus served as daily transportation from the sunniest to the snowiest of days. In 2000, after much soul searching, Ron sold his treasured ride.

Although Bus-less now, in the summertime, Ron, his wife, and their daughter are occasionally nestled in an orange and blue Westfalia tent among the green mountains of Vermont. If you happen by their campfire, you might hear fondly told tales of journeys on the road with their beloved VW Bus.

Clara Williams (I Was Hauling In My Bus One Day)

Clara is the artisan behind Panels by Clara (Instagram: @panelsbyclara), a VW Bus parts reproduction business in California. She is also immersed in restoring an old farmhouse that had a lot of "deferred maintenance" by the previous owners.

Marek Zebrowski (Our Anniversary)

Marek Zebrowski was born in Poznan, Poland, and began studying piano at the age of five. After graduating with the highest honors from the Poznan Music Lyceum, he went to France, where he was a pupil of Robert Casadesus and Nadia Boulanger. Mr. Zebrowski came to the United States in 1973 and continued his studies of piano with Russell Sherman at the New England Conservatory of Music, where he received his bachelor's and master's degrees. Marek is Director of the Polish Music Center, University of Southern California, and collaborated with David Lynch on the film, *Inland Empire*.

Glossary

A large variety of Type 2's were built. The VW factory often supplied basic vehicle bodies to outside companies that converted them into everything from touring buses, cherry-pickers, firetrucks, campers, even hearses. For the purposes of this book, we'll stick to the most common terms. (For more details, see *VW Transporter and Microbus: Specification Guide 1950-1967.*)

The VW Bus acquired a lot of different names over the years. Some have very specific meanings, and some are generic, some can be both. This list is not exhaustive.

Generic:

Bus, Van, Microbus, Transporter, Type 2, Splitty (in reference to the divided front windshields).

Specific:

Barndoor: So named because of the *very large* engine lid. Type 2's built 1950 through early 1955. Quite rare.

Kombi & panel van: The least adorned of models offered. One color paint, either no side windows (panel), or 3 side windows on each side.

Single Cab & Double Cab: Most similar to "pick-up trucks," with the added feature of fold-down side and rear gates that create a flatbed for transporting whatever fits. Not as common as other models.

Deluxe: The VW Bus with the most added extras. There are two versions of Deluxe: The solid roof model, and the "samba" or sunroof model (with the additional 8 oval roof windows). Depending on the model year, there are two variations of the variations: The solid roof Deluxe came as 11-window, or

13-window (the 13 window includes two rear corner windows). The sunroof models came as either 21-window, or 23-window (the 23 window includes two rear corner windows).

Of special note: Sunroofs could sometimes be found on Kombi models.

Westfalia (Westy): The German company that converted the VW Bus into campers. There have been several different companies (in Germany, Canada, the U.S., and elsewhere) that camperized VW Buses, but this brand is the most commonly seen.

Brazilian Bus: Brazilian Buses are *different*. The VW factory in Brazil built the split-window style until 1975, with various unique features.

Bay/Bay window: Denotes Type 2's built with one large windshield, starting in 1968.

Vanagon: The North American moniker for Type 2's built 1979-1991. The first couple years of this design used air-cooled motors.

Wasserboxer: Water-cooled, rather than air-cooled Vanagons starting in 1982 with diesel engines, and 1983 until end of production with gasoline engines.

Suggested Reading & Internet Resources

Lago, John (aka Johnny Bock). *A Bus Will Get You There.* Oshkosh, WI: Lunchbreak Press. The author vividly describes the joys and tribulations of owning and driving an old VW Bus (the same VW Bus!) from the 1960's to the present. A must-read.

Eccles, David. *VW Camper, The Inside Story: A Guide to the Various Camping Conversions and Interior Layouts Used for VW Campers 1951-2005.* 2006. Ramsbury, Marlborough, UK: The Crowood Press. Ltd.

Eccles, David. *VW Transporter and Microbus: Specification Guide 1950-1967.* 2004. The Crowood Press, UK.

Eccles, David and Cee. *Campervan Crazy: Travels with My Bus—a Tribute to the VW Camper and the People Who Drive Them.* 2006. London: Kyle Cathie, Ltd. US Edition: *Traveling with the VW Bus and Camper.* 2007. New York; Abbeville Press.

qFiasco, Flash. *Welcome to the Crumple Zone.* 2006. Darlington, UK: Serendipity Press.

Schlüter, Christian. *111 VW Bus Stories That You Should Know.* The VW Bus is not just a car. It is sentimental, a part of the family. A way of life on wheels. That's why most of them have names. And almost everyone has some sort of connection to the VW Bus. This book offers fascinating stories about one of the most popular automobiles of all time and the most successful camper van in the world—a kaleidoscope from the world of VW Buses.

Steinke, Michael. *VW-Campingwagen, 1951-1991.* 2003. Stuttgart: Schrader Verlag. Michael Steinke has a vast collection of VW Bus-related literature. This 95-page book reprints many

German-language factory brochures from Westfalia, and a few other VW camper conversion manufacturers. Nearly all reprints and all commentary written in German. Great photos throughout.

Websites

There are many great websites to learn more about VW Buses. Since this book will reach mainly the English-speaking world, I recommend: TheSamba.com. This site will connect you to almost everywhere you want to go.